Practising Gramı

Workbook 2

Jon Blundell

Nelson

Thomas Nelson and Sons Ltd
Nelson House   Mayfield Road
Walton-on-Thames   Surrey
KT12 5PL   UK

51 York Place
Edinburgh
EH1 3JD   UK

Thomas Nelson (Hong Kong) Ltd
Toppan Building 10/F
22A Westlands Road
Quarry Bay   Hong Kong

First published by Thomas Nelson and Sons Ltd 1989

ISBN 0–17–555742–X

NPN 9 8 7 6 5 4 3

Illustrated by Hilary Norman

Printed in Hong Kong.

Contents

1

Questions with the present simple —————————

1 Complete the letter from Dimitri to his English pen-friend. This list will help you. Write two more questions yourself.

LIST

1 live in a town?
3 your house have a garden?
5 your mother have a job?
7 drink a lot of tea?
9 have a bicycle?
11 like pop music?
13 have a personal stereo?
15 do homework every day?
17 your family have a car?

2 have a big house?
4 have any brothers or sisters?
6 your family have any pets?
8 watch television every day?
10 collect stamps?
12 play a musical instrument?
14 like your school?
16 speak a second language?
18 have a computer?

19 ————————————————— ? *20* ————————————————— ?

Ermou 28,
Thessaloniki,
8th June

Dear Tom,

Hallo! I hope you're O.K. This is my English homework! My friends and I have a long list of questions for you. I hope you can answer them. Here they are:

1 Do you live in a town? _____ 2 _____
3 _____ 4 _____
5 _____ 6 _____
7 _____ 8 _____
9 _____ 10 _____
11 _____ 12 _____
13 _____ 14 _____
15 _____ 16 _____
17 _____ 18 _____
19 _____ 20 _____

Best wishes

Dimitri

2 You sent a letter to Belinda. This is her reply. What questions did you ask her? The asterisks (*) will help you.

28, Ralton Road,
Abingdon,
Oxfordshire.
22nd June.

Hi!

Thanks for your letter. Here are my answers to your questions.
*I live in Abingdon, near Oxford. *I get up at 7 o'clock in the morning, *have breakfast at 7.30, and *leave for school at 8.15. *I go to school by car. *My Dad takes me there, and *school starts at 9 o'clock. *My favourite lesson is English, and *Miss Johnson, the English teacher is my favourite teacher. *My best friend's name is Diana. *My hobbies are stamp-collecting and photography.
*My Dad works in a garage. *My brother doesn't do anything. *He's only six months old, so *he doesn't have a job!

Bye for now,

Belinda

Example: **Where do you live?**

1 _____
2 _____
3 _____
4 _____
5 _____
6 _____
7 _____
8 _____
9 _____
10 _____
11 _____
12 _____
13 _____
14 _____

3 Professor Nemo discovered a new sea animal yesterday. Newspaper reporters are asking him questions. What do they ask?

Examples:

dangerous?   **_Is it dangerous?_**

Where/live?   **_Where does it live?_**

1 What/eat? _____

2 eat fish? _____

3 eat people? _____

4 How/breathe? _____

5 How/swim? _____

6 have/teeth? _____

7 intelligent? _____

8 attack people? _____

9 When/attack people? _____

10 Why/have three eyes? _____

11 change colour? _____

12 Why/change colour? _____

13 Why/looking at us? _____

14 Why/climbing out of its tank? _____

14

Questions with the past simple

4 Complete these conversations.

Examples:

A: **_Did you find_** your pen?

B: Yes, I found it, thanks.

A: **_Where did you go_** last night?

B: I went to my friend's house.

1 A: _____ _____ _____ TV yesterday?

    B: No, TV's boring. I never watch it.

2 A: _____ _____ _____ _____ on Saturday?

    B: We went to a football match.

3 A: _____ _____ _____ Peter?

   B: Yes, but he wasn't in. I can phone again, later.

4 A: _____ _____ _____ your bed this morning?

   B: Yes. I make it every morning.

5 A: _____ _____ _____ _____ _____ this morning?

   B: At seven o'clock. I always get up at seven o'clock.

6 A: _____ _____ _____ _____ to school yesterday?

   B: By bus. I always go by bus.

7 A: _____ _____ _____ my letter?

   B: Yes, I posted it last night.

8 A: _____ _____ _____ _____ on Saturday?

   B: A record. I bought a new record.

9 A: _____ _____ _____ to Alan's birthday party?

   B: No, I didn't go. I was ill.

10 A: _____ _____ _____ your English exam?

   B: Yes, of course I passed. It was easy!

2

Comparison of adjectives ━━━━━━━━━━━━━━━

Comparative of adjectives with one syllable + *er* + *than*

Note the exceptions: good – **better** / bad – **worse**

1 Complete these sentences.

Example: warm   Athens is ***warmer than*** Moscow.

1   cold   Alaska is _____ _____ Texas.

2   high   Mount Everest is _____ _____ Mount Parnassus.

3   tall   The Empire State Building is _____ _____ the Eiffel Tower.

4   short   Pygmies are _____ _____ other people.

5   old   The Egyptian pyramids are _____ _____ Greek temples.

6   young   The earth is _____ _____ the sun.

7   small   Hens' eggs are _____ _____ ducks' eggs.

8   rich   The USA is _____ _____ Canada.

9   poor   Arizona is _____ _____ Alabama.

10 new   Astronomy is _____ _____ astrology.

11 quick   Jet planes are _____ _____ propeller-driven planes.

12 slow   Steam trains are _____ _____ diesel trains.

13 long   The Amazon is _____ _____ the Danube.

14 fast   Racing cars can go _____ _____ sports cars.

15 good   Medical knowledge today is _____ _____ it was fifty years ago.

16 bad   Pollution is _____ _____ it was fifty years ago.

16

Adjectives like this double the consonant in the comparative form:

big – bi**gg**er / fat – fa**tt**er

2 Complete these sentences.

Example: big   Whales are ***bigger than*** elephants.

1   hot   Summer is _____ _____ spring.

2   wet   The west of England is _____ _____ the east.

3   thin   Fashion models are usually _____ _____ other people.

4   fat   Eating lots of chocolates makes you _____ _____ eating fruit.

4

8

Superlative of adjectives with one syllable + est

Note:	good	–	**best**	big	–	biggest
	bad	–	**worst**	fat	–	fattest

3 Look at the table on the right and complete the sentences with an adjective in the superlative form.

Example: The ___**biggest**___ mammal in the world is the whale.

1 The _____ mountain in the world is Mount Everest.

2 The _____ place in the world is in the Arctic.

3 The _____ animal in the world is the tortoise.

4 The _____ place in the world is in Hawaii.

5 The _____ river in the world is the Nile.

6 The _____ desert in the world is the Sahara.

7 The _____ language in the world is Chinese.

8 The _____ bird in the world is the humming bird.

9 The _____ planet to Earth is Venus.

10 The _____ animal in the world is the cheetah.

11 The _____ building in the world is the Sears Building in Chicago.

12 The _____ lake in Britain is Loch Morar.

cold
fast
large
high
old
wet
near
deep
small
long
(big)
slow
tall

4 Complete Tom's letter. Use the comparative or superlative form of: *bad, big, cold, good, high, new, old, rich, wet*. Write in *the* and *than* where necessary.

Royal Hotel,
Edinburgh.
7th May.

Dear Pavlos,

     I'm in Scotland now. It's <u>colder</u> and <u>wetter than</u> in England. We're staying at _____ be___ hotel in Edinburgh. It's bi___ and ne_____ _____ our hotel in London. Only ___ ri_____ people stay here! We visited St Andrews yesterday. It's _____ ol___ university in Scotland. Tomorrow I'm going to Ben Nevis, ___ hi___ mountain in Scotland. I hope the weather gets be___. It's_____ w _____ weather for twelve years!

        Bye Tom.

B

Comparative and superlative of adjectives with two syllables

> Comparative with **er** + **than** and superlative with **the** + **est**
>
> *Remember:* adjectives which end in **y** change **y** to **i**
>
> clever – clever**er** – the clever**est**
>
> pretty – prett**i**er – the prett**i**est
>
> lazy – laz**i**er – the laz**i**est
>
> noisy – nois**i**er – the – the nois**i**est
>
> friendly – friendl**i**er – the friendl**i**est

5 Write sentences. Use the adjectives in the box below.

clever	noisy	funny	friendly	lazy

Example:

Peter is lazier than Mike, but Steve is the laziest

boy in the class.

_____

1

_____

_____

_____ girl in the family.

2

_____

_____

_____ programme on TV.

10

3

_____

_____

_____ baby in the room.

4

_____

_____

_____ person in the office.

Comparative and superlative of adjectives with three syllables

Comparative with **more** and superlative with **the most**

Example: intelligent – **more** intelligent – **the most** intelligent.

6 Alpha, Beta and Gamma are three new planets.
What do we know about them?

		Alpha	Beta	Gamma
1 Intelligent beings		X	X X	X X X
2 Terrible storms		X X X	X	X X
3 Beautiful mountains		X X	X X X	X
4 Dangerous animals		X	X X X	X X
5 Difficult language		X X X	X X	X
6 Horrible insects		X X	X	X X X

Example:

1 **The beings on Beta are more intelligent than on Alpha, but those on Gamma are the**
most intelligent.

2 _____

3 _____   4 _____

5 _____   6 _____

Comparison with *as . . . as . . .*

As + adjective + as: *Example:*   Kate's *as* intelligent *as* Linda.

Not as + adjective + as: *Example:*   Kate's *not as* intelligent *as* Teresa.

7 **How good are Simon, Andreas and Mario at these sports?**
   Answer the questions.

Example: How good is Andreas at playing football?

He's as good as Mario, but he's not as good as Simon.

1 How good is Mario at swimming?

_____

2 How good is Simon at basketball?

_____

3 How good is Mario at tennis?

_____

4 How good is Andreas at table-tennis?

_____

5 How good is Mario at golf?

_____

Adjectives with too, enough

too + adjective   /   *not* + adjective + *enough*

8 Complete with *too* or *not enough.*

Example: water   /   hot?

A: **Is the water too hot?**
B: **No, it's not hot enough.**

1 television   /   loud?

A: _____

_____

B: _____

_____

2 we go   /   fast?

A: _____

_____

B: _____

_____

13

3 ladder / long?

A: _____

_____

B: _____

_____

4 dress / big?

A: _____

_____

B: _____

_____

5 exam / difficult?

A: _____

_____

B: _____

_____

10

3

Present perfect of regular verbs

To form the present perfect we use *have* and the *past participle*.

Affirmative

Long form	Short form
I have finished you have finished he/she/it has finished we/you/they have finished	I've finished you've finished he's/she's/it's finished we've/you've/they've finished

1 Complete.

Example: film/start

	Long form	Short form
	The film has started.	*The film's started.*
1 lesson/finish.		
2 Bill and Peter/arrive.		
3 we/wash all the dishes.		
4 I/clean my bicycle.		
5 she/open the envelope.		
6 I/listen to my new record.		
7 Tom/repair the television.		
8 Anna/ask Dave to her party.		
9 I/answer her letter.		
10 Sue/type the report.		

Negative

Long form	Short form
I have not finished you have not finished he/she/it has not finished we/you/they have not finished	I haven't finished you haven't finished he/she/it hasn't finished we/you/they haven't finished

2 Complete.

Example: Peter/not wash car.

	Long form	Short form
	Peter has not washed the car.	*Peter hasn't washed the car.*
1 I/not open your letter.		

	Long form	Short form
2 They/not answer my note.		
3 The football match/not start.		
4 Karen/not ask to leave school early.		
5 We/not clean our shoes.		
6 They/not repair the stereo.		
7 Your new bike/not arrive.		
8 I/not finish my coffee.		
9 Jill/not listen to your new cassette.		
10 John/not phone Mike.		

10

Questions and short answers
Have you finished? – Yes, I have./No, I haven't.

3 Look at the lists and continue the conversation.

Mum	Dad
1 Clean kitchen	1 Wash car ✓
2 Wash hair ✓	2 Paint bathroom
3 Post letters	3 Repair electric fire ✓
4 Repair vacuum-cleaner ✓	4 Phone the garage
5 Start new book	5 Watch football match on TV ✓

Example:

1 Mum: **Have you washed the car?**

Dad: **Yes, I have.**

Dad: **Have you cleaned the kitchen?**

Mum: **No, I haven't.**

2 Mum: _____

Dad: _____

Dad: _____

Mum: _____

3 Mum: _____

Dad: _____

Dad: _____

Mum: _____

4 Mum: _____

Dad: _____

Dad: _____

Mum: _____

5 Mum: _____

Dad: _____

Dad: _____

Mum: _____

Present perfect of irregular verbs

Long form	Short form	Questions and short answers
I have won you have won he/she/it has won we/you/they have won	I've won you've won he's/she's/it's won we've/you've/they've won	Have you won? – Yes I have. No, I haven't.

4 Complete the sentences. Use participles from this table.

Past participles					
been	bought	broken	come	done	drunk
eaten	found	gone	had	lost	made
read	seen	sold	taken	won	written

Examples:

Tom (win) the race.   ***Tom has won the race.***

Matthew (not eat) his sandwiches.   ***Matthew hasn't eaten his sandwiches.***

you (write) to your pen-friend?   ***Have your written to your pen-friend?***

1 Who (take) my keys?

_____

2 They (not do) their English homework.

_____

3 Karen (sell) her camera.

_____

4 you (see) Emma's new dress?

_____

5 I (break) my glasses.

_____

6 The postman (not come) yet.

_____

7 We (be) in New York for two weeks.

_____

8 you (buy) Tony a birthday present?

_____

9 Sally (not find) her handbag.

_____

10 Peter (go) to bed yet?

_____

11 I (make) you a cup of tea.

_____

12 We (not have) a letter from Nick for two months.

_____

13 you (read) the newspaper?

_____

14 They (lose) their luggage.

_____

15 The cat (not drink) its milk.

_____

Ever and never

| Examples: | Have you **ever** been to England? | Yes, I have. |
| | Have you **ever** been to China? | No, we haven't. We've **never** been to China. |

**5 Write fourteen different sentences from this table.
Use _you_ (x4), _your friend_ (x5) and your parents (x5).**

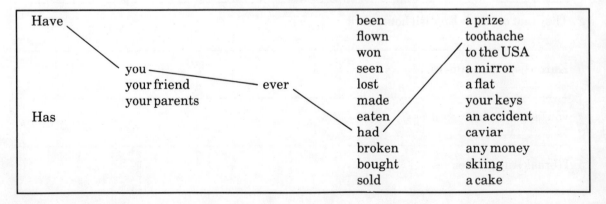

Example: **Have you ever had toothache?**

1 _____

2 _____

3 _____

4 _____

5 **Has your friend . . .**

6 _____

7 _____

8 _____

9 _____

10 **Have your parents . . .**

11 _____

12 _____

13 _____

14 _____

6 Now *answer* the questions in Exercise 5.

Example: Have you ever had toothache?

No, I haven't. I've never had toothache.

1 _____

2 _____

3 _____

4 _____

5 _____

6 _____

7 _____

8 _____

9 _____

10 _____

11 _____

12 _____

13 _____

14 _____

7 Complete the crossword.

CLUES

Across

2 I've (break) **_broken_** the window.

3 Dave's (make) _____ the tea.

4 We've (sell) _____ our car.

5 Have you (do) _____ your homework?

6 Tom hasn't (come) _____ yet.

9 Anna's (buy) _____ a new record.

10 Bill's (drink) _____ his coffee.

13 Have you (win) _____ any money?

14 I've never (have) _____ a bicycle.

15 Peter's (be) _____ ill.

Down

1 I've (find) _____ my books.

4 Have you (see) _____ our new house?

7 Who's (eat) _____ my sandwiches?

8 Anna's (lose) _____ her handbag.

11 I haven't (read) _____ the newspaper yet.

12 Sarah and Tessa have (go) _____ to a party.

15

4

Present perfect with just, yet, already, nearly ⎯⎯

Just

> *Example:* have/has + just + past participle:
> They have *just* arrived.

1 Complete these sentences.

Example: The plane/just land.

The plane has just landed.

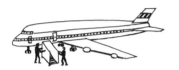

1

The film/just end.

_____

_____

2

We/just score a goal!

_____

_____

3

She/just finish breakfast.

_____

_____

4

They/just catch the bus.

_____

_____

5

The train/just leave the station.

_____

_____

6

It/just stop raining.

_____

_____

7

The race/just start.

_____

_____

8

They/just escape from prison.

_____

_____

9

They/just break a window.

_____

_____

10

She/just make a cake.

_____
_____

11

He/just sell the car.

_____
_____

12

She/just buy a record.

_____
_____

13

They/just do the washing-up.

_____
_____

14

He/just find his keys.

_____
_____

15

They/just go for a swim.

_____
_____

15

Yet

Example: Have they arrived **yet?**/Yes, they have.

2 Look back at Exercise 1 and complete these conversations.

Example:

A: _**Has the plane landed yet?**_

B: _**Yes, it has.**_

_1_ A: _____

B: _____

_2_ A: _____

B: _____

_3_ A: _____

B: _____

_4_ A: _____

B: _____

_5_ A: _____

B: _____

_6_ A: _____

B: _____

7 A: _____
  B: _____

8 A: _____
  B: _____

9 A: _____
  B: _____

10 A: _____
   B: _____

11 A: _____
   B: _____

12 A: _____
   B: _____

13 A: _____
   B: _____

14 A: _____
   B: _____

15 A: _____
   B: _____

Not yet

Example: He has**n't** had his breakfast *yet*.

3 What has the nurse done/just done/not yet done?

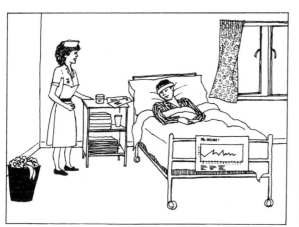

Mr Walker

Take his temperature	– Yes.
Make his bed	– Not yet.
Check his pulse	– Yes.
Give him his pills	– Just.
Fill in his chart	– Not yet.
Change his bandages	– Not yet.
Bring him his letters	– Just.
Tidy his room	– Yes.
Open the window	– Yes.
Empty the wastepaper basket	– Not yet.

Example:

She's taken his temperature.

She hasn't made his bed yet.

1 _____

2 _____

3 _____

4 _____

5 _____

6 _____

7 _____

8 8 _____

Already

> *Example:*   He's **already** written it.

4 Write answers using the present perfect and *already*.

Example: Don't forget to do your English homework!

I've already done it.

1 Don't lose your key!

_____

_____

2 Remember to write that letter!

_____

_____

3 Don't forget to close the window!

_____

_____

4 Don't open your birthday present *now*!

_____

_____

5 Clean your bike!

_____

_____

6 Drink your coffee!

_____

_____

7 Have your breakfast!

_____

_____

8 Don't miss the bus!

_____

_____

9 Don't eat the last cake!

_____

_____

10 Make your bed!

_____

_____

10

Nearly

> *Example:*   We've ***nearly*** finished.

5 Look at the pictures and write sentences.

Example: The exam/finish.

The exam's nearly finished.

1

He/win the race.

_____

_____

2

The match/end.

_____

_____

3

They/finish lunch.

_____

_____

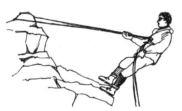

4

He/reach the top.

_____

_____

5

She/do her English homework.

_____

_____

6

He/break the world record.

_____

_____

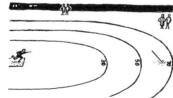

7

She/throw it seventy metres.

_____

_____

8

They/finish their books.

_____

_____

c

5

Present perfect/past simple

1 **You are on holiday with your parents in London. You have just met a new English friend. You have been in London for a week. Look at the list of places and complete the conversation.**

Tower of London	– (Monday)
Buckingham Palace	– (Wednesday morning)
Oxford Street	– (Friday morning)
National Gallery	– (Tuesday morning)
Houses of Parliament	– (Thursday)
Westminster Abbey	– (Wednesday afternoon)
Hyde Park	– (Yesterday)
St Paul's Cathedral	– (Friday afternoon)

Example:

A: **Have you been to the Tower of London?**

B: **Yes. We went there on Monday.**

1 A: _____

  B: _____

2 A: _____

  B: _____

3 A: _____

  B: _____

4 A: _____

  B: _____

5 A: _____

  B: _____

6 A: _____

  B: _____

14 7 A: _____

  B: _____

2 Stavros is also on holiday in London. Today is Thursday, his fourth day. Look at the list and make sentences.

HOLIDAY IN LONDON

Visit the Tower of London ✓ (Monday morning)

See Westminster Abbey (Not yet)

Visit the National Gallery ✓ (Monday afternoon)

Go to the Houses of Parliament ✓ (Tuesday morning)

Have a picnic in Hyde Park (Not yet)

See Tower Bridge (Tuesday afternoon)

Take a photo of Nick outside Buckingham Palace (Not yet)

See St. Paul's Cathedral (Not yet)

Go to the Science Museum (Wednesday morning)

See the famous ship the 'Victory' (Not yet)

Example:

He visited the Tower of London on Monday morning.

He hasn't seen Westminster Abbey yet.

1 _____

2 _____

3 _____

4 _____

5 _____

6 _____

7 _____

8 _____

3 Harry and Charlie are in London for one day. It's now two o'clock in the afternoon. What have they done so far today? What haven't they done yet? Look at the numbers on the map.

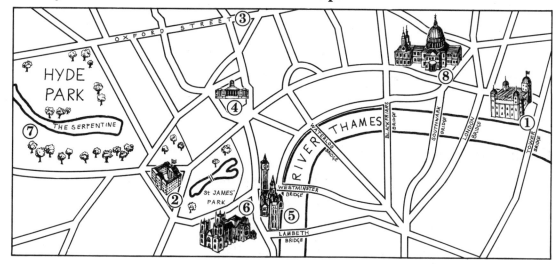

Example: They (visit) number 8.

They've visited St. Paul's Cathedral.

1 They (not see) number 6.

_____

2 Harry (take) a photograph of Charlie outside number 5.

_____

3 They (not visit) number 4 yet.

_____

4 They just (listen) to a brass band in number 7.

_____

5 They (spend) hundreds of dollars in number 3.

_____

6 They (not see) the Queen at number 2 yet.

_____

7 Harry just (have) two hamburgers in number 7.

_____

8 Charlie just (buy) number 1!

8

4 Harry and Charlie are back in the USA now. Charlie is telling his wife what they did/didn't do. Write what Charlie said about each place.

Example: **We visited St. Paul's Cathedral.**

1 _____

2 _____

3 _____

4 _____

5 _____

6 _____

7 _____

8 8 _____

5 Complete these conversations.

Example: A: ever (go) to Germany?   **Have you ever been to Germany?**

B: Yes.   **Yes, I have.**

A: Where (go)?   **Where did you go?**

B: (go) to the Black Forest.   **I went to the Black Forest.**

1 A: ever (go) skiing?

B: Yes.

A: Where (go)?

B: (go) to France.

2 A: ever (go) to a pop concert.

B: Yes.

A: Who (see)?

B: (see) Michael Jackson.

3 A: ever (use) a computer?

B: Yes.

A: When (use) it?

B: (use) one last week at school.

4 A: ever (eat) octopus?

B: Yes.

A: What (be) it like?

B: It (be) delicious!

5 A: ever (fly) in an aeroplane?

B: Yes.

A: Where (fly) to?

B: (fly) on holiday to Rome.

6 A: ever (see) an elephant?

B: Yes.

A: Where (see) it?

B: (see) one on television!

7 A: ever (catch) a fish?

B: Yes.

A: When (catch) it?

B: (catch) one last Saturday.

8 A: ever (have) an eye-test?

B: Yes.

A: When (have) it?

B: (have) one last year.

9 A: ever (go) on a camping holiday? _____

    B: Yes. _____

    A: Where (go)? _____

    B: (go) to Scotland. _____

Past simple + ago

Example:		
I **wrote** to my brother in Australia three weeks **ago**	two years ago	two days ago
	three months ago	three hours ago
	six weeks ago	five minutes ago

6 Duncan Cameron is a famous explorer. How long ago did he do these things?

Example: **1977:**   find three Spanish treasure ships.

He found three Spanish treasure ships twelve years ago.

1 **1970:** discover the lost tombs of the Pharaohs.

_____

_____

_____

2 **1978:** find the lost treasure of the Incas.

_____

_____

_____

3 **1980:** discover the oldest dinosaur.

_____

_____

_____

4 **1982:** capture a *yeti* in the Himalayas.

_____

_____

_____

5 **1983:** catch the Loch Ness Monster.

_____

_____

_____

6 **1985:** climb Mount Everest.

_____

_____

_____

12

7 Hans Schmidt is also a great explorer. He doesn't like Duncan Cameron. He claims he did everything one year before Cameron. Complete this interview.

Interviewer: Professor Schmidt, you say you did everything before Mr Cameron.

Professor: Yes. I *discovered* the lost tomb of the Pharoahs _____1 years _____2.

I f_____3 the lost treasure of the Incas _____4 years _____5.

I dis_____6 the oldest dinosaur _____7 years _____8.

Interviewer: I see. All exactly one year before. Very interesting! And the *yeti*? Did you capture a *yeti* before Mr Cameron?

Professor: Yes. Of course, I did. I ca_____9 a *yeti* _____10 years _____11. And in 1982 I ca_____12 the Loch Ness Monster! That was _____13 years _____14.

Interviewer: But why didn't we hear about all these discoveries in the newspapers, on the radio, on television?

Professor: I'm a shy man. I don't like publicity!

Interviewer: I see. But Mount Everest, you didn't climb Mount Everest before Mr Cameron, did you?

Professor: Yes. _____15 years _____16. Twice! Sorry, I have to go now. I've got another interview to do for the BBC!

8 Write down something that happened in the past.

Example: three years ago

I went on holiday to Scotland three years ago.

1 two years ago

_____

2 six months ago

_____

3 two weeks ago

_____

4 two days ago

_____

5 five minutes ago

_____

6

Present perfect with for, since

Present perfect + *for* (a period of time)

1 Bob borrows things from his friends, but he forgets to give them back. He still has all these things. How long has he had them?

Example: keep Tania's record – 3 weeks

He's kept Tania's record for three weeks.

1 have Peter's pen   –   2 months.

_____

2 borrow Anne's cassette player   –   6 weeks.

_____

3 keep Dave's cassettes   –   4 weeks.

_____

4 have Alan's computer game   –   a month.

_____

5 borrow Tom's tennis racket   –   3 months.

_____

6 keep Kate's camera   –   5 weeks.

_____

7 have Nicola's chess-set   –   6 months.

_____

8 borrow Helen's English dictionary   –   3 weeks.

_____

2 Think of ten things that you or your friends or family have. How long have you/they had them?

Examples:

I've had my cassette player for two years.   We've had our washing-machine for three years.

Tom's had his motorbike for three months.

1 _____

2 _____

3 _____

4 _____

5 _____

6 _____

7 _____

8 _____

9 _____

10 _____

Present perfect + *since* (a point in time)

3 Complete these conversations.

Example:　Johnny live in Texas – 1940.

A: ***How long has Johnny lived in Texas?***

B: ***Since 1940. He's lived in Texas since 1940.***

1

Kenny Denton/play for Liverpool – 1982.

A: _____

_____

B: _____

_____

2

Mick Dyson/be a boxer – 1984.

A: _____

_____

B: _____

_____

3

Jill Carfax/play in the New York Symphony Orchestra – August.

A: _____

_____

B: _____

_____

4 Tatyana Krachnikova / dance with the Bolshoi Ballet – 1983.

A: _____

_____

B: _____

_____

5 Ricky Clifton / have a Rolls Royce – May 1983.

A: _____

_____

B: _____

_____

6 Jim Finnigan / have a broken nose – last summer.

A: _____

_____

B: _____

_____

7 Alberto Manzini / hold the world championship – 1987.

A: _____

_____

B: _____

_____

8 Butch Hernandez / play for the Chicago Bears – last year.

A: _____

_____

B: _____

_____

8

4 Look back at Exercise 2. Write your ten sentences again, but this time use *since* + a point in time.

Examples:

I've had my cassette-player since 1988.   *We've had our washing-machine since 1987.*

Tom's had his motorbike since July.

1 _____

2 _____

3 _____

4 _____

5 _____

6 _____

7 _____

8 _____

9 _____

10 _____

> Present perfect + **for** + period of time
> + **since** + point in time

5 Kirsty and her husband Mike are on holiday in Tahira. They arrived on the island on the 1st August. Use Kirsty's notes to complete her letter to her friend Sue.

1 The rain (not stop) – six days
2 We (stay) in the hotel – the day we came
3 Mike (feel) sick – three days
4 He (not eat) – two days
5 I (have) a cold – Thursday
6 We (not understand) a word of Tahiran – we arrived!

Example: We (be) on Tahira – Tuesday

We've been on Tahira since Tuesday.

Tahira,
7ᵗʰ August.

Dear Sue,

We've been on Tahira since Tuesday and we're having a dreadful time. It's cold and wet here and the rain (1) _____.
(2) _____. What a holiday! Mike
(3) _____ . (4) _____.
(5) _____. We both feel awful.
And we (6) _____.

Have a nice time in Querino!

            Love
                Kirsty.

6

6 **Chris has eight girlfriends! Today they all telephoned him from different places. Where are they? How long have they been there? Complete the conversations.**

Anna	–	Paris/two days
Lisa	–	London/three days
Caroline	–	Rome/a week
Nicola	–	Madrid/four days
Belinda	–	Athens/five days
Helen	–	Frankfurt/three hours
Jill	–	Amsterdam/six days
Kate	–	Venice/three days

Example:

Chris: **Hallo? Anna? Where are you?**

Anna: **I'm in Paris.**

Chris: **Paris? How long have you been there?**

Anna: **I've been here for two days.**

1 Chris: _____

Lisa: _____

Chris: _____

Lisa: _____

2 Chris: _____

Caroline: _____

Chris: _____

Caroline: _____

3 Chris: _____

Nicola: _____

Chris: _____

Nicola: _____

4 Chris: _____

Belinda: _____

Chris: _____

Belinda: _____

5 Chris: _____

Helen: _____

Chris: _____

Helen: _____

6 Chris: _____

   Jill: _____

   Chris: _____

   Jill: _____

7 Chris: _____

   Kate: _____

   Chris: _____

28   Kate: _____

For/since

7 Complete these sentences. Use *for* or *since*.

Example: I – a teacher / three years.

I'm a teacher. I've been a teacher for three years.

1 Mr Carter – pilot / 1983.

   _____

2 Dr Benson – doctor / two years.

   _____

3 Miss Clark – secretary / three months.

   _____

4 Mr Bond – dentist / last July.

   _____

5 Mr Denver – mechanic / three years.

   _____

6 Melissa – pop singer / five months.

   _____

7 Linda Langton – film star / thirty years.

   _____

8 Ted Clarke – postman / 1985.

   _____

9 Tessa Jones – photographer / October.

   _____

10 10 Jonathan – engineer / 1970.

   _____

7

Much/many

Negative

1 Complete the sentences.

Example:

There aren't many bananas.

There isn't much butter.

1

_____ cake.

2

_____ apples.

3

_____ tea.

4

_____ sandwiches.

5

_____ coffee.

6

_____ lemonade.

7

_____ grapes.

8

_____ sugar.

9

_____ chocolates.

10

_____ Coke.

11

_____ orangeade.

12

_____ oranges.

A lot of

Examples: There's *a lot of* butter in the fridge.

There *are a lot of apples* in the drawer.

2 Write sentences. Use *there's a lot of* or *there are a lot of*.

Examples:

snow on the mountains.

There's a lot of snow on the mountains.

snakes in the jungle.

There are a lot of snakes in the jungle.

1   sand in the desert.

_____

2   water in the Great Lakes.

_____

3   forests in Canada.

_____

4   elephants in Africa.

_____

5   sheep in Australia.

_____

6   lakes in North America.

_____

7   ice in the Arctic.

_____

8   islands around Greece.

_____

9   oil in the Middle East.

_____

10   gold in South Africa.

_____

3 Write the conversations.

Use: **much / many / a lot of**.

Examples:

Anna/friends?

A: *Has Anna got many friends?*

B: *No, she hasn't got many.*

C: *Yes, she has! She's got a lot of friends!*

she/money?

A: *Has she got much money?*

B: *No, she hasn't got much.*

C: *Yes, she has! She's got a lot of money!*

1 she/hobbies?

   A: _____

   B: _____

   C: _____

2 she/books?

   A: _____

   B: _____

   C: _____

3 she/English homework this evening?

   A: _____

   B: _____

   C: _____

4 she/records?

   A: _____

   B: _____

   C: _____

5 she/time to listen to her records?

   A: _____

   B: _____

   C: _____

6 she/jewellery?

   A: _____

   B: _____

18   C: _____

Answer key

Unit 1

1　1 Do you live in a town?　2 Do you have a big house?　3 Does your house have a garden?　4 Do you have any brothers or sisters?　5 Does your mother have a job?　6 Do/Does your family have any pets?　7 Do you drink a lot of tea?　8 Do you watch television every day?　9 Do you have a bicycle?　10 Do you collect stamps?　11 Do you like pop music?　12 Do you play a musical instrument?　13 Do you have a personal stereo?　14 Do you like your school?　15 Do you do homework every day?　16 Do you speak a second language?　17 Does your family have a car?　18 Do you have a computer?　19 *Students' own answers.*　20 *Students' own answers.*

2　1 When/What time do you get up?　2 When/What time do you have breakfast?　3 When/What time do you leave for school?　4 How do you go to school?　5 Who takes you there?　6 When/What time does school start?　7 What is your favourite lesson?　8 Who is your favourite teacher?　9 What is your best friend's name?　10 What are your hobbies?　11 Where does your Dad work?　12 What does your brother do?　13 How old is he?　14 Does he have a job?

3　1 What does it eat?　2 Does it eat fish?　3 Does it eat people?　4 How does it breathe?　5 How does it swim?　6 Does it have teeth?　7 Is it intelligent?　8 Does it attack people?　9 When does it attack people?　10 Why does it have three eyes?　11 Does it change colour?　12 Why does it change colour?　13 Why is it looking at us?　14 Why is it climbing out of its tank?

4　1 Did you watch　2 Where did you go　3 Did you phone/ring　4 Did you make　5 When did you get up　6 How did you go　7 Did you post　8 What did you buy　9 Did you go　10 Did you pass

Unit 2

1　1 colder than　2 higher than　3 taller than　4 shorter than　5 older than　6 younger than　7 smaller than　8 richer than　9 poorer than　10 newer than　11 quicker than　12 slower than　13 longer than　14 faster than　15 better than　16 worse than.

2　1 hotter than　2 wetter than　3 thinner than　4 fatter than.

3　1 highest　2 coldest　3 slowest　4 wettest　5 longest　6 largest　7 oldest　8 smallest　9 nearest　10 fastest　11 tallest　12 deepest.

4　1 the best　bigger and newer than　the richest　the oldest　the highest　better　the worst.

5　1 Jenny is cleverer than Sally, but Lucy is the cleverest girl in the family.　2 *The Busby Show* is funnier than *Keep Smiling*, but *A Laugh a Minute* is the funniest programme on TV.　3 Joe is noisier than Joanna, but Jessie is the noisiest baby in the room.　4 John is friendlier than Sara, but Colin is the friendliest person in the office.

6　1 The beings on Beta are more intelligent than on Alpha, but those on Gamma are the most intelligent.　2 The storms on Gamma are more terrible than on Beta, but those on Alpha are the most terrible.　3 The mountains on Alpha are more beautiful than on Gamma, but those on Beta are the most beautiful.　4 The animals on Gamma are more dangerous than on Alpha, but those on Beta are the most dangerous.　5 The language on Beta is more difficult than on Gamma, but that on Alpha is the most difficult.　6 The insects on Alpha are more horrible than on Beta, but those on Gamma are the most horrible.

7　1 He's as good as Simon, but he's not as good as Andreas.　2 He's as good as Andreas, but he's not as good as Mario.　3 He's as good as Simon, but he's not as good as Andreas.　4 He's as good as Simon, but he's not as good as Mario.　5 He's as good as Andreas, but he's not as good as Simon.

8　1 Is the television too loud?/No, it's not loud enough.　2 Are we going too fast?/No, we're not going fast enough.　3 Is the ladder too long?/No, it's not long enough.　4 Is the dress too big?/No, it's not big enough.　5 Is the exam too difficult?/No, it's not difficult enough.

Unit 3

1　1 The lesson has finished./The lesson's finished.　2 Bill and Peter have arrived./Bill and Peter've arrived.　3 We have washed all the dishes./We've washed all the dishes.　4 I have cleaned my bicycle./I've cleaned my bicycle.　5 She has opened the envelope./She's opened the envelope.　6 I have listened to my new record./I've listened to my new record.　7 Tom has repaired the television./Tom's repaired the television.　8 Anna has asked Dave to her party./Anna's asked Dave to her party.　9 I have answered her letter./I've answered her letter.　10 Sue has typed the report./Sue's typed the report.

2　1 I have not opened your letter./I haven't opened your letter.　2 They have not answered my note./They haven't answered my note.　3 The football match has not started./The football match hasn't started.　4 Karen has not asked to leave school early./Karen hasn't asked to leave school early.　5 We have not cleaned our shoes./We haven't cleaned our shoes.　6 They have not repaired the stereo./They haven't repaired the stereo. 7 Your new bike has not arrived./Your new bike hasn't arrived. 8 I have not finished my coffee./I haven't finished my coffee. 9 Jill has not listened to your new cassette./Jill hasn't listened to your new cassette. 10 John has not phoned Mike./John hasn't phoned Mike.

3 1 Mum: Have you painted the bathroom?
    Dad: No, I haven't.
    Dad: Have you washed your hair?
    Mum: Yes, I have.

  2 Mum: Have you repaired the electric fire?
    Dad: Yes I have.
    Dad: Have you posted the letters?
    Mum: No, I haven't.

  3 Mum: Have you phoned the garage?
    Dad: No, I haven't.
    Dad: Have you repaired the vacuum-cleaner?
    Mum: Yes, I have.

  4 Mum: Have you watched the football match on TV?
    Dad: Yes. I have.
    Dad: Have you started your new book?
    Mum: No, I haven't.

4 1 Who has taken my keys? 2 They haven't done their English homework. 3 Karen has sold her camera. 4 Have you seen Emma's new dress? 5 I have broken my glasses. 6 The postman hasn't come yet. 7 We have been in New York for two weeks. 8 Have you bought Tony a birthday present? 9 Sally hasn't found her handbag. 10 Has Peter gone to bed yet? 11 I have made you a cup of tea. 12 We haven't had a letter from Nick for two months. 13 Have you read the newspaper? 14 They have lost their luggage. 15 The cat hasn't drunk its milk.

5 *Suggested answers:* 1 Have you ever broken a mirror? 2 Have you ever lost your keys? 3 Have you ever won any money? 4 Have you ever eaten caviar? 5 Has your friend ever had an accident? 6 Has your friend ever made a cake? 7 Has your friend ever been skiing? 8 Has your friend ever sold a flat? 9 Has your friend ever had toothache? 10 Have your parents ever seen an accident? 11 Have your parents ever won a prize? 12 Have your parents ever lost any money? 13 Have you parents ever bought a flat? 14 Have your parents ever flown to the USA?

6 *Students' own answers.*

7 Across: 3 MADE 4 SOLD 5 DONE 6 COME 9 BOUGHT 10 DRUNK 13 WON 14 HAD 15 BEEN.
Down: 1 FOUND 4 SEEN 7 EATEN 8 LOST 11 READ 12 GONE.

Unit 4

1 1 The film has just ended. 2 We've just scored a goal! 3 She's just finished breakfast. 4 They've just caught the bus. 5 The train has just left the station. 6 It's just stopped raining. 7 The race has just started. 8 They've just escaped from prison. 9 They've just broken a window. 10 She's just made a cake. 11 He's just sold the car. 12 She's just bought a record. 13 They've just done the washing-up. 14 He's just found his keys. 15 They've just been for a swim.

2 1 Has the film ended yet?/Yes, it has. 2 Have we scored a goal yet?/Yes, we have. 3 Has she finished breakfast yet?/Yes, she has. 4 Have they caught the bus yet?/Yes, they have. 5 Has the train left the station yet?/Yes, it has. 6 Has it stopped raining yet?/Yes, it has. 7 Has the race started yet?/Yes, it has. 8 Have they escaped from prison yet?/Yes, they have. 9 Have they broken a window yet?/Yes, they have. 10 Has she made a cake yet?/Yes, she has. 11 Has he sold the car yet?/Yes, he has. 12 Has she bought a record yet?/Yes, she has. 13 Have they done the washing-up yet?/Yes, they have. 14 Has he found his keys yet?/Yes, he has. 15 Have they been for a swim yet?/Yes they have.

3 1 She's checked his pulse. 2 She's just given him his pills. 3 She hasn't filled in his chart yet. 4 She hasn't changed his bandages yet. 5 She's just brought him his letters. 6 She's tidied his room. 7 She's opened the window. 8 She hasn't emptied the wastepaper basket yet.

4 1 I've already lost it. 2 I've already written it. 3 I've already closed it. 4 I've already opened it. 5 I've already cleaned it. 6 I've already drunk it. 7 I've already had it. 8 I've already missed it. 9 I've already eaten it. 10 I've already made it.

5 1 He's nearly won the race. 2 The match has nearly ended. 3 They've nearly finished lunch. 4 He's nearly reached the top. 5 She's nearly done her English homework. 6 He's nearly broken the world record. 7 She's nearly thrown it seventy metres. 8 They've nearly finished their books.

Unit 5

1 1 Have you been to Buckingham Palace/Yes, we went there on Wednesday morning. 2 Have you been to Oxford Street?/Yes, we went there on Friday morning. 3 Have you been to the National Gallery?/Yes, we went there on Tuesday morning. 4 Have you been to the Houses of Parliament?/Yes, we went there on Thursday. 5 Have you been to Westminster Abbey?/Yes, we went there on Wednesday afternoon. 6 Have you been to Hyde Park?/Yes, we went there yesterday? 7 Have you been to St. Paul's

Cathedral?/Yes, we went there on Friday
afternoon.

2 *1* He visited the National Gallery on Monday
afternoon.   *2* He went to the Houses of
Parliament on Tuesday morning.   *3* He hasn't
had a picnic in Hyde Park yet.   *4* He saw Tower
Bridge on Tuesday afternoon.   *5* He hasn't taken
a photo of Nick outside Buckingham Palace yet.
6 He hasn't seen St. Paul's Cathedral yet.   *7* He
went to the Science Museum on Wednesday
morning.   *8* He hasn't seen the famous ship The
Victory yet.

3 *1* They haven't seen Westminster Abbey.
2 Harry has taken a photograph of Charlie
outside the Houses of Parliament. *3* They
haven't visited the National Gallery yet.
4 They've just listened to a brass band in
Hyde Park.   *5* They've spent hundreds of
dollars in Oxford Street.   *6* They haven't seen the
Queen at Buckingham Palace yet.   *7* Harry's just
had two hamburgers in Hyde Park.   *8* Charlie's
just bought the Tower of London!

4 *1* We didn't see Westminster Abbey.   *2* Harry
took a photograph of me outside the Houses of
Parliament.   *3* We didn't visit the National
Gallery.   *4* We listened to a brass band in Hyde
Park.   *5* We spent hundreds of dollars in Oxford
Street.   *6* We didn't see the Queen at
Buckingham Palace.   *7* Harry had two
hamburgers in Hyde Park.   *8* I bought the Tower
of London!

5 *1* A: Have you ever been skiing?
  B: Yes, I have.
  A: Where did you go?
  B: I went to France.

2 A: Have you ever been to a pop concert?
  B: Yes, I have.
  A: Who did you see?
  B: I saw Michael Jackson.

3 A: Have you ever used a computer?
  B: Yes, I have.
  A: When did you use it?
  B: I used one last week at school.

4 A: Have you ever eaten octopus?
  B: Yes, I have.
  A: What was it like?
  B: It was delicious!

5 A: Have you ever flown in an aeroplane?
  B: Yes, I have.
  A: Where did you fly to?
  B: I flew on holiday to Rome.

6 A: Have you ever seen an elephant?
  B: Yes, I have.
  A: Where did you see it?
  B: I saw one on television!

7 A: Have you ever caught a fish?
  B: Yes, I have.

A: When did you catch it?
B: I caught one last Saturday.

8 A: Have you ever had an eye-test?
  B: Yes, I have.
  A: When did you have it?
  B: I had one last year.

9 A: Have you ever gone on a camping holiday?
  B: Yes, I have.
  A: Where did you go?
  B: I went to Scotland.

6 *Note: The number of years has been left blank as
the answers will depend on when the exercise is
completed.*   *1* He discovered the lost tombs of the
Pharaohs . . . years ago.   *2* He found the lost
treasure of the Incas . . . years ago.   *3* He
discovered the oldest dinosaur . . . years ago.
4 He captured a *yeti* in the Himalayas . . . years
ago.   *5* He caught the Loch Ness Monster . . .
years ago.   *6* He climbed Mount Everest . . .
years ago.

7 *See note to exercise 6. The number of 'years ago'
will be one more than for the previous exercise as
Schmidt claims that he did everything one year
before Cameron.*   *1* . . .   *2* ago   *3* found   *4* . . .
5 ago   *6* discovered   *7* . . .   *8* ago   *9* captured
10 . . .   *11* ago   *12* caught   *13* . . .   *14* ago
15 . . .   *16* ago.

8 *Students' own answers.*

Unit 6

1 *1* He's had Peter's pen for two months.   *2* He's
borrowed Anne's cassette player for six weeks.
3 He's kept Dave's cassettes for four weeks.
4 He's had Alan's computer game for a
month.   *5* He's borrowed Tom's tennis racket
for three months.   *6* He's kept Kate's camera
for five weeks.   *7* He's had Nicola's chess-set
for six months.   *8* He's borrowed Helen's
English dictionary for three weeks.

2 *Students' own answers*

3 *1* How long has Kenny Denton played for
Liverpool?/Since 1982. He's played for Liverpool
since 1982.   *2* How long has Mick Dyson been a
boxer?/Since 1984. He's been a boxer since
1984.   *3* How long has Jill Carfax played in the
New York Symphony Orchestra?/Since August.
She's played in the New York Symphony
Orchestra since August.   *4* How long has
Tatyana Krachnikova danced with the Bolshoi
ballet?/Since 1983. She's danced with the Bolshoi
ballet since 1983.   *5* How long has Ricky Clifton
had a Rolls Royce?/Since May 1983. He's had a
Rolls Royce since May 1983.   *6* How long has Jim
Finnigan had a broken nose?/Since last summer.
He's had a broken nose since last summer.
7 How long has Alberto Manzini held the world
championship?/Since 1987. He's held the world

championship since 1987.   *8* How long has Butch Hernandez played for the Chicago Bears?/Since last year. He's played for the Chicago Bears since last year.

4 *Students' own answers*

5 *1* hasn't stopped for six days.   *2* We've stayed in the hotel since the day we came.   *3* Mike's felt sick for three days.   *4* He hasn't eaten for two days.   *5* I've had a cold since Thursday.
6 I haven't understood a word of Tahiran since we arrived!

6 *1*
Chris:	Hallo? Lisa? Where are you?
Lisa:	I'm in London.
Chris:	London? How long have you been there?
Lisa:	I've been here for three days.

2
Chris:	Hallo? Caroline? Where are you?
Caroline:	I'm in Rome.
Chris:	Rome? How long have you been there?
Caroline:	I've been here for a week.

3
Chris:	Hallo? Nicola? Where are you?
Nicola:	I'm in Madrid.
Chris:	Madrid? How long have you been there?
Nicola:	I've been here for four days.

4
Chris:	Hallo? Belinda? Where are you?
Belinda:	I'm in Athens.
Chris:	Athens? How long have you been there?
Belinda:	I've been here for five days.

5
Chris:	Hallo? Helen? Where are you?
Helen:	I'm in Frankfurt.
Chris:	Frankfurt? How long have you been there?
Helen:	I've been here for three hours.

6
Chris:	Hallo? Jill? Where are you?
Jill:	I'm in Amsterdam.
Chris:	Amsterdam? How long have you been there?
Jill:	I've been here for six days.

7
Chris:	Hallo? Kate? Where are you?
Kate:	I'm in Venice.
Chris:	Venice? How long have you been there?
Kate:	I've been here for three days.

7 *1* Mr Carter's been a pilot since 1983.
2 Dr Benson's been a doctor for two years.
3 Miss Clark's been a secretary for three months.
4 Mr Bond's been a dentist since last July.
5 Mr Denver's been a mechanic for three years.
6 Melissa's been a pop singer for five months.
7 Linda Langton's been a film star for thirty years.   *8* Ted Clarke's been a postman since 1985.   *9* Tessa Jones has been a photographer since October.   *10* Jonathan's been an engineer since 1970.

Unit 7

1 *1* There isn't much cake.   *2* There aren't many apples.   *3* There isn't much tea.   *4* There aren't many sandwiches.   *5* There isn't much coffee.
6 There isn't much lemonade.   *7* There aren't many grapes.   *8* There isn't much sugar.
9 There aren't many chocolates.   *10* There isn't much Coke.   *11* There isn't much orangeade.
12 There aren't many oranges.

2 *1* There's a lot of sand in the desert.   *2* There's a lot of water in the Great Lakes.   *3* There are a lot of forests in Canada.   *4* There are a lot of elephants in Africa.   *5* There are a lot of sheep in Australia.   *6* There are a lot of lakes in North America.   *7* There's a lot of ice in the Arctic.
8 There are a lot of islands around Greece.
9 There's a lot of oil in the Middle East.
10 There's a lot of gold in South Africa.

3 *1* Has she got many hobbies?/No, she hasn't got many./Yes, she has! She's got a lot of hobbies!
2 Has she got many books?/No, she hasn't got many./Yes, she has! She's got a lot of books!
3 Has she got much English homework this evening?/No, she hasn't got much./Yes she has! She's got a lot of English homework!   *4* Has she got many records?/No, she hasn't got many./Yes, she has! She's got a lot of records!   *5* Has she got much time to listen to her records?/No, she hasn't got much./Yes, she has! She's got a lot of time!
6 Has she got much jewellery?/No, she hasn't got much./Yes, she has! She's got a lot of jewellery!

4 *1* She's got lots of hobbies.   *2* She's got lots of books.   *3* She's got lots of English homework.
4 She's got lots of records.   *5* She's got lots of time to listen to her records.   *6* She's got lots of jewellery.

5 *1* A little cake.   *2* A few sandwiches.   *3* A little tea.   *4* A few oranges.   *5* A little sugar.   *6* A few bananas.   *7* A little lemonade.   *8* A few chocolates.   *9* A little Coke.   *10* A few grapes.
11 A little coffee.   *12* A little water.   *13* A few snakes.   *14* A little sand.   *15* A few elephants.
16 A little ice.   *17* A little oil.   *18* A few islands.   *19* A few books.   *20* A few photos.
21 A little food.   *22* A little snow.   *23* A little luggage.   *24* A few lakes.   *25* A little petrol.
26 A little gold.   *27* A little money.   *28* A few forests.

Unit 8

1 *1* *Suggested answers:*   *1* He was playing a cassette.   *2* You were writing a letter.   *3* They were digging the garden.   *4* You were reading your letter.   *5* They were doing their homework.   *6* It was drinking its milk.   *7* He was robbing the bank.   *8* They were playing football.   *9* He was making a sandwich.   *10* We were doing the washing-up.   *11* She was listening to the cassette.   *12* She was reading your letter.   *13* I was making a cake.   *14* He was having a sandwich.   *15* We were listening to your cassette.

2   *1* The cat was dreaming of a fish/sleeping.   *2* Bob was washing the windows.   *3* Ann was writing.   *4* Kate was reading.   *5* Sally and Tessa were talking.   *6* Dave was drinking a cup of tea.   *7* Mick was reading the notice board.   *8* Andy and Tony were playing chess.   *9* Diana was eating a banana.   *10* Gary was making a phone call.

3   *1* Was the cat dreaming of a fish?/Yes, it was.   *2* Was Bob eating a sandwich?/No, he wasn't.   *3* Was Gary washing the windows?/No, he wasn't.   *4* Was Ann writing?/Yes, she was.   *5* Were Sally and Tessa talking?/Yes, they were.   *6* Was Diana eating a banana?/Yes, she was.   *7* Was Kate reading the notice board.   /No, she wasn't.   *8* Was Mick playing football?   /No, he wasn't.   *9* Was Dave drinking a cup of tea?/Yes, he was.   *10* Were Andy and Tony playing chess?/Yes, they were.

4   *Suggested answers:*   *1* The cat wasn't drinking a cup of tea.   *2* Bob wasn't eating a sandwich.   *3* Ann wasn't making a phone call.   *4* Kate wasn't writing.   *5* Sally and Tessa weren't playing chess.   *6* Dave wasn't reading.   *7* Mick wasn't eating a banana.   *8* Andy and Tony weren't washing windows.   *9* Diana wasn't reading the notice board.   *10* Gary wasn't dreaming of a fish.

5   *1* The rain started when we were playing football.   *2* Anna was watching television when her father came home.   *3* Tony was having lunch when the letter arrived.   *4* The lights went out when they were doing their homework.   *5* We saw the car crash when we were walking to school.   *6* Bill was smoking a cigarette when the teacher came in.   *7* The bell rang for the end of the lesson when the teacher was speaking.

6   *1* She was running to work when she dropped her purse.   *2* Kate found her camera when she was tidying her room.   *3* The phone rang when Pete was mending his bicycle.   *4* The postcard arrived when Nick was having lunch.   *5* It started to snow when they were climbing the mountain.   *6* We were sitting in the classroom when the teacher arrived.   *7* He was crossing the road when he fell over.   *8* My mother arrived when I was watching the news.

7   *1* She dropped her purse when she was running to work.   *2* When she was tidying her room, Kate found her camera.   *3* When Pete was mending his bicycle the phone rang.   *4* When Nick was having lunch the postcard arrived.   *5* When they were climbing the mountain it started to snow.   *6* When the teacher arrived we were sitting in the classroom.   *7* He fell over when he was crossing

the road.   *8* When I was watching the news my mother arrived.

Unit 9

1   *1* He still trains young basketball players.   *2* He used to practise six hours a day.   *3* He used to run a hundred metres in 10.5 seconds.   *4* He still appears on television in sports quizzes.   *5* He used to go on long world tours with his team.   *6* He still visits his old school to give talks on basketball.   *7* He used to go hang-gliding at weekends.   *8* He still enjoys watching a good game on television.

2   *1* A: Did he use to train young basketball
                players?
         B: Yes, he did.
         A: Does he do that now?
         B: Yes, he does.

    2 A: Did he use to practise six hours a day?
         B: Yes, he did.
         A: Does he do that now?
         B: No, he doesn't.

         A: Did he use to run a hundred metres in 10.5
                seconds?
         B: Yes, he did.
         A: Does he do that now?
         B: No, he doesn't.

    4 A: Did he use to appear on television in sports
                quizzes?
         B: Yes, he did?
         A: Does he do that now?
         B: Yes, he does.

    5 A: Did he use to go on long world tours with
                his team?
         B: Yes, he did.
         A: Does he do that now?
         B: No, he doesn't.

    6 A: Did he use to visit his old school to give
                talks on basketball?
         B: Yes, he did.
         A: Does he do that now?
         B: Yes, he does.

    7 A: Did he use to go hang-gliding at
                weekends?
         B: Yes, he did.
         A: Does he do that now?
         B: No, he doesn't.

    8 A: Did he use to enjoy watching a good game
                on television.
         B: Yes, he did.
         A: Does he do that now?
         B: Yes, he does.

3   *1* didn't use to   *2* used to   *3* used to   *4* didn't use to   *5* didn't use to   *6* didn't use to   *7* used to   *8* didn't use to.

4 *1* Mr Curtiss used to be a mechanic, but now he's a farmer. *2* Mrs Curtiss used to be a typist, but now she helps on the farm. *3* Steve Curtiss used to be unemployed, but now he's studying at agricultural college. *4* They didn't use to have a dog, but now they have three sheep dogs. *5* Sally, the baby, used to cry a lot, but now she's much happier. *6* Emma didn't use to have many friends, but now she's got lots of friends. *7* Mr Curtiss used to smoke a lot, but now he doesn't smoke at all. *8* The weather in England didn't use to be good, but in Australia the weather's wonderful. *9* They didn't use to have an Australian accent, but now they have strong Australian accents. *10* They didn't use to enjoy life, but now they enjoy life very much.

5 *Suggested answers:* *1* There used to be a church where the railway station is. *2* There didn't use to be a railway station. *3* There used to be a wood where the Newton Housing Estate is. *4* There didn't use to be a housing estate. *5* There used to be an orchard where the M4 motorway is. *6* There didn't use to be a motorway. *7* There used to be a ford where the bridge is. *8* There didn't use to be a bridge. *9* There used to be a water mill. *10* There didn't use to be a cinema.

6 *Students' own answers.*

Unit 10

1 *1A* Hudson controls the ball better, runs faster and shoots harder than Spinetti.
1B Spinetti controls the ball better and kicks the ball further than Muller. Muller passes the ball earlier, jumps higher, runs faster and shoots harder than Spinetti.
1C Hudson controls the ball better, runs faster and shoots harder than Muller. Muller passes the ball earlier, kicks the ball further and jumps higher than Hudson.

2 I think Hudson is 'Footballer of the Year' because he controls the ball best, runs fastest and shoots hardest.

3 *1* worse *2* worse *3* worst *4* badly *5* badly *6* worst.

4 *1* King makes his moves more quickly than Capelli, thinks more deeply than Markov, prepares his matches more carefully than Capelli or Markov, but gets angry more easily than Capelli or Markov. *2* Markov plans his moves more intelligently than King, makes his moves more quickly than King or Capelli, but gets angry more easily than Capelli.

5 *1* most *2* easily *3* most *4* intelligently *5* the *6* most *7* deeply *8* more *9* quickly *10* more *11* easily *12* most *13* carefully *14* most *15* deeply *16* most *17* intelligently *18* more *19* carefully *20* than *21* easily.

6 *1* earlier than *2* more carefully than *3* later than *4* more efficiently than *5* faster than *6* more quickly *7* worse than *8* more easily than.

Unit 11

1 *1* Excuse me is this yours?/No, it's mine. *2* Excuse me are those cases yours? No, they're not ours. I think they're hers. *3* Flight BA 162. That's ours! *4* No, his hasn't landed yet. *5* No, it isn't. Theirs is two hours late.

2 *1* She's the woman who phoned yesterday. *2* That's the athlete who won the gold medal. *3* Where's the typist who typed my letter? *4* That's the waiter who served us. *5* These are the children who broke the window. *6* Where's the tourist who lost his passport? *7* These are the students who arrived today. *8* Are you the person who wanted to see me?

3 *1* Those are the tourists whose luggage arrived late. *2* That's the girl whose photograph I saw in the paper *3* Here are the passengers whose plane was delayed. *4* That's the woman whose passport you found. *5* That's the pop star whose record went to number one. *6* Those are the fishermen whose boat sank yesterday. *7* Maria is the girl whose brother is in hospital. *8* You're the man whose brother I met at Anna's party!

4 *1* We have a compass that/which always points south, a matchbox that/which has no matches in it, and boots that/which don't fit. But at least we have a tin opener that/which works, and a tent that/which doesn't let the rain in.

5 *1* The photographs you took are very good. *2* He's the man we saw in the hotel. *3* Are those the chocolates I bought? *4* Here's the cassette you lost. *5* Sally's the person you want to see. *6* The doctor we saw was very good. *7* The music they played at the disco was awful. *8* The hotel we stayed at was great.

6 *1* The photographs that you took are very good. *2* He's the man who we saw in the hotel. *3* Are those the chocolates that I bought? *4* Here's the cassette that you lost. *5* Sally's the person who you want to see. *6* The doctor who we saw was very good. *7* The music that they played at the disco was awful. *8* The hotel that we stayed at was great.

Unit 12

1 *1* Dry Dry Dry will be there. *2* Princess won't be there. She'll be in Rome. *3* Nanarama will be there. *4* Red Red Red won't be there. They'll be in Moscow. *5* Girls at Work won't be there. They'll be in Athens. *6* Rod Elton and Cliff Stewart will be there. *7* Sarah and the Royals won't be there. They'll be in Paris. *8* Charlie and the Wailers will be there.

2 *1* Will Dry Dry Dry be there?/Yes, they will.
2 Will Princess be there?/No, she won't. She won't be there. *3* Will Nanarama be there?/Yes, they will. *4* Will Red Red Red be there?/No, they won't. They won't be there. *5* Will Girls at Work be there?/No, they won't. They won't be there. *6* Will Red Elton and Cliff Stewart be there?/Yes, they will. *7* Will Sarah and the Royals be there?/No, they won't. They won't be there. *8* Will Charlie and the Wailers be there?/Yes, they will.

3 *1* will *2* will *3* Will *4* won't *5* won't *6* will *7* won't *8* 'll *9* 'll *10* 'll.

4 *1* arriving *2* 're staying *3* 're planning *4* 're going *5* 're visiting *6* 're going *7* 're arriving *8* 're flying.

5 *1* Mr Parker's going home on Wednesday.
No, he isn't. That's Friday. He isn't going home until Friday.

2 Mrs Walker's having her blood test this morning.
No, she isn't. That's this afternoon. She isn't having her blood test until this afternoon.

3 Miss Stanton's seeing the physiotherapist on Monday.
No, she isn't. That's Wednesday. She isn't seeing the physiotherapist until Wednesday.

4 Mr Cobb's seeing a specialist on Tuesday.
No, he isn't. That's Thursday. He isn't seeing a specialist until Thursday.

5 Mrs Trenchard's starting new treatment on Thursday.
No, she isn't. That's Saturday. She isn't starting new treatment until Saturday.

6 *1* Am I going home on Wednesday? No./When am I going home then?/On Friday. *2* Am I having my blood-test this morning?/No./When am I having it then?/This afternoon. *3* Am I seeing the physiotherapist on Monday?/No./When am I seeing him (her) then?/On Wednesday. *4* Am I seeing a specialist on Tuesday?/No./When am I seeing him (her) then?/On Thursday. *5* Am I starting new treatment on Thursday?/No./When am I starting it, then?/On Saturday.

Unit 13

1 *1* 'll wait/stops *2* ends/'ll complain *3* 'll stay/leaves *4* 'll worry/gets *5* gets/'ll want *6* won't start/get *7* arrives/'ll give *8* 's/'ll have *9* 'll have/starts *10* 'll finish/go.

2 *1* b *2* a *3* b *4* a *5* b *6* a *7* a *8* b *9* a *10* a.

3 *1* 'll phone/land *2* 'll send/leave *3* won't open/is *4* get/'ll cook *5* 'll sell/breaks down *6* 'll see/comes *7* 'll stay/arrive *8* 'll type/go.

4 *1* If Jenny gets a new job she'll meet interesting people. *2* If it rains we'll drive to the party *3* If John gets up at eight o'clock he'll be late for

work. *4* If they don't work hard they won't pass their exams. *5* If she loses her umbrella she'll buy a new one. *6* If I don't eat biscuits I'll lose weight. *7* If Jim moves house he'll be near the station. *8* If my brother goes to France this summer he won't be here for my birthday.

5 *1* score(s)/'ll win *2* will come/ask *3* 'll play/practise *4* lend/'ll fall *5* don't come/will be *6* won't get/doesn't pass *7* 's/won't catch *8* 'll have/go.

6 *1* If she jumps off, she'll hurt herself. *2* If she rings the bell, no one will hear her. *3* If she turns left, she'll run over the children. *4* If she turns right, she'll crash into the lorry. *5* If she doesn't do anything, she'll go into the pond. *6* If she goes into the pond, she'll get very wet. *7* If she doesn't do something soon, it'll be too late. *8* If she stops in time, it'll be a miracle!

Unit 14

1 *1* We've got to work late this evening. *2* I must mend this hosepipe. *3* We've got to cut the grass. *4* I've got to tidy my room. *5* We must do something about that noise. *6* The doctor says I've got to go into hospital tomorrow. *7* I must get some food before the shops close. *8* I've got to do the washing-up.

2 *1* Why do I have to be home by ten o'clock?
2 Have we got to tell Sue? *3* Has he got to walk to work? *4* When do we have to leave? *5* Have you got to work at weekends? *6* Who does she have to ask, then? *7* When do they have to book their tickets? *8* Where have I got to wait?

3 *1* She should/ought to go to the dentist.
2 They should/ought to leave immediately.
3 She should/ought to phone the police.
4 She should/ought to phone the bank.
5 He should/ought to go to bed earlier.
6 She should/ought to have an eye-test.
7 He should/ought to buy a new one.
8 He should/ought to take more exercise.
9 He should/ought to wait until his birthday.
10 He should/ought to drive more carefully.

4 *1* She should read the questions carefully. *2* She shouldn't write too much. *3* She should answer all the questions. *4* She should write clearly.
5 She shouldn't cheat.

5 *1* He ought to prepare some questions to ask.
2 He ought to put on a smart suit. *3* He oughtn't to worry too much. *4* He ought to have a haircut. *5* He oughtn't to be late!

6 *1* They should choose a good language school.
2 They oughtn't to speak Italian when they get to England. *3* They oughtn't to spend too much money in the first month. *4* They should write to or phone their families every week. *5* They should take their umbrellas.

1 *1* myself   *2* yourself   *3* themselves   *4* itself
5 ourselves   *6* yourselves   *7* herself   *8* himself.

2 *1* The climber couldn't stop himself.   *2* Don't hurt
yourselves on those new skateboards.   *3* Paul's
cut himself shaving.   *4* You've bruised yourself
badly.   *5* Andreas is teaching himself English.
6 Colin's cut himself on the glass.

3 *1* Fire-eater burns himself.   *2* 'I couldn't stop
myself,' says murderer.   *3* 'Enjoy yourself while
you're young.'   *4* Fourteen-year-old boy teaches
himself Chinese in three months.

4 *1* He's picking the letters up.   *2* She's plugging
the iron in.   *3* She's switching/putting the
television on.   *4* He's putting his coat on.   *5* He's
switching/putting the light off.   *6* They're putting
their records away.

5 *1* Pick up the letters!/I've picked them up.   *2* Plug
the iron in!/I've plugged it in.   *3* Switch/Put the
television on!/I've switched/put it on.   *4* Put your
coat on!/I've put it on.   *5* Switch/Put the light off/
I've switched/put it off.   *6* Put your records away!/
We've put them away.

6 *1* got up   *2* jumped out   *3* Go away   *4* fell down
5 came in   *6* run away   *7* drove away   *8* sat
down.

7 *1* up   *2* on   *3* on   *4* off   *5* up   *6* down/away
7 off   *8* down.

Lots of in affirmative sentences.

**4 Look back at Exercise 4. We can use *lots of* instead of *a lot of*.
Write sentences.**

Example: Anna's got lots of friends.

1 _____

2 _____

3 _____

4 _____

5 _____

6 _____

A little/a few

   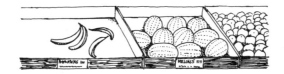

A *little* butter   **A *few* bananas**

5 Complete this list.

Examples:

A little butter.   **A few apples.**

1 _____ cake.	2 _____ sandwiches.	3 _____ tea.
4 _____ oranges.	5 _____ sugar.	6 _____ bananas.
7 _____ lemonade.	8 _____ chocolates.	9 _____ Coke.
10 _____ grapes.	11 _____ coffee.	12 _____ water.
13 _____ snakes.	14 _____ sand.	15 _____ elephants.
16 _____ ice.	17 _____ oil.	18 _____ islands.
19 _____ books.	20 _____ photos.	21 _____ food.
22 _____ snow.	23 _____ luggage.	24 _____ lakes.
25 _____ petrol.	26 _____ gold.	27 _____ money.
28 _____ forests.		

8

Past continuous

Affirmative

I was playing
you were playing
he was playing
she was playing
it was playing
we were playing
you were playing
they were playing

Remember these two types of verbs:

1   have + ing   =   having   *2*   stop + ing   =   sto**pp**ing
      write + ing   =   writing   rob + ing   =   ro**bb**ing
      make + ing   =   making   dig + ing   =   di**gg**ing

1   Make fifteen sentences. Use *all* of the words in the table.

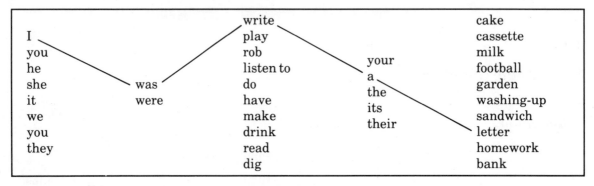

I	write		cake
you	play		cassette
he	rob	your	milk
she	listen to	a	football
it	was	do	the	garden
we	were	have	its	washing-up
you	make	their	sandwich
they	drink		letter
	read		homework
	dig		bank

Example: **I was writing a letter.**

1 _____
2 _____
3 _____
4 _____
5 _____
6 _____
7 _____
8 _____
9 _____
10 _____
11 _____
12 _____

13 _____

14 _____

15 _____

2 Look at the picture. What *were they doing* when the fire alarm rang?

> *Use these verbs:*   **make** (phone call), **dream** (of), **drink, eat, play** (football), **play** (chess),
> **read, talk, wash, write.**

Example: Bill and Tom *were playing football.*

1 The cat _____

2 Bob _____

3 Ann _____

4 Kate _____

5 Sally and Tessa _____

6 Dave _____

7 Mick _____

8 Andy and Tony _____

9 Diana _____

10 Gary _____

Questions

Was I playing?
Were you playing?
Was he/she/it playing?
Were we playing?
Were you playing?
Were they playing?

Short answers

Yes, I was.   No, I wasn't.
Yes, you were.   No, you weren't.
Yes, he/she/it was.   No, he/she/it wasn't.
Yes, we/you/they were.   No, we/you/they weren't.

3 Write questions and answers. Look back at the picture in Exercise 2 for the answers.

Example: Bill and Tom/have lunch?

A: *__Were Bill and Tom having lunch?__*

B: *__No, they weren't.__*

1 cat/dream of a fish?

A: _____

B: _____

2 Bob/eat a sandwich?

A: _____

B: _____

3 Gary/wash the windows?

A: _____

B: _____

4 Ann/write?

A: _____

B: _____

5 Sally and Tessa/talk?

A: _____

B: _____

6 Diana/eat a banana?

A: _____

B: _____

7 Kate/read the notice board?

A: _____

B: _____

8 Mick/play football?

A: _____

B: _____

9 Dave/drink a cup of tea?

A: _____

B: _____

10 Andy and Tony/play chess?

A: _____

B: _____

Negative

I was not (wasn't) playing	we were not (weren't) playing
you were not (weren't) playing	you were not (weren't) playing
he/she/it was not (wasn't) playing	they were not (weren't) playing

4 Write ten sentences about what was *not* happening in the picture.

Example: **Bill and Tom weren't playing chess.**

1 _____

2 _____

3 _____

4 _____

5 _____

6 _____

7 _____

8 _____

9 _____

10 _____

Past simple/past continuous

We use the past continuous for *interrupted* actions and the past simple for *completed* actions.

Past continuous + *when* + past simple

I **was having** a shower when my friend **telephoned**.

Past simple + *when* + past continuous

My friend **telephoned** when I **was having** a shower.

5 Make sentences. Sometimes you need to start with the past simple and sometimes with the past continuous.

Example: I (have) a shower/my friend telephone.

I was having a shower when my friend telephoned.

1 The rain (start)/we (play) football.

_____

2 Anna (watch) television/her father (come) home.

_____

3 Tony (have) lunch/the letter (arrive).

_____

4 The lights (go) out/they (do) their homework.

_____

5 We (see) the car crash/we (walk) to school.

_____

6 Bill (smoke) a cigarette/the teacher (come) in.

_____

7 The bell (ring) for the end of the lesson/the teacher (speak).

_____

14

6 Find the sentences!

Example: to France they crashed plane flying their when were

They were flying to France when their plane crashed.

1 she purse running was to work when she her dropped

_____

2 camera was Kate found tidying room her she when her

_____

3 when Pete mending rang the phone bicycle his was

_____

4 the Nick postcard was arrived having lunch when

_____

5 climbing started they to snow it were mountain the when

_____

6 were classroom the the teacher sitting arrived when we in

_____

7 he road the crossing when he fell over was

_____

8 watching mother I the when was arrived news my

_____

7 Now write your sentences the other way round.

Example: **Their plane crashed when they were flying to France.**

1 _____

2 _____

3 _____

4 _____

5 _____

6 _____

7 _____

8 _____

9

Used to *for past habits*

> *used to* + verb
>
> *Examples:* I ***used to*** play the guitar.
>
> They ***used to*** practise every day.

Past habit/present habit

> *Example:* I ***used to*** get up at six o'clock but now I get up at seven o'clock.

1 **Andy Newman, the famous basketball player has retired from world-class basketball. Look at the list below. What things do you think he used to do? What do you think he still does?**

> LIST
>
> Run ten miles before breakfast.
> Write for *Basketball Sports Magazine*.
> Train young basketball players.
> Practise six hours a day.
> Run hundred metres in 10.5 seconds.
> Appear on television in sports quizzes.
> Go on long world tours with his team.
> Visit his old school to give talks on
>   basketball.
> Go hang-gliding at weekends.
> Enjoy watching a good game on television.

Examples:

He used to run ten miles before breakfast.

He still writes for Basketball Sports Magazine.

1 _____

2 _____

3 _____

4 _____

5 _____

6 _____

7 _____

8 | 8 _____

Questions and short answers

Did she **use to** walk to school?	Yes, she did.
Did they **use to** play football?	No, they didn't.

2 Look back at the list in Exercise 1 and make questions and answers about Andy Newman.

Example:

A: **Did he use to run ten miles before breakfast?**

B: **Yes, he did.**

A: **Does he do that now?**

B: **No, he doesn't.**

Example:

A: **Did he use to write for Basketball Sports Magazine?**

B: **Yes, he did.**

A: **Does he do that now?**

B: **Yes, he does.**

1 A: _____

    B: _____

    A: _____

    B: _____

2 A: _____

    B: _____

    A: _____

    B: _____

3 A: _____

    B: _____

    A: _____

    B: _____

4 A: _____

    B: _____

    A: _____

    B: _____

5 A: _____

   B: _____

   A: _____

   B: _____

6 A: _____

   B: _____

   A: _____

   B: _____

7 A: _____

   B: _____

   A: _____

   B: _____

8 A: _____

   B: _____

   A: _____

32

   B: _____

Didn't use to

> *didn't use to* + verb
>
> *Examples:* We ***didn't use to*** play tennis at school.
>
>   I ***didn't use to*** go to work by bus.

3 Mr Bates is visiting his doctor. Complete the conversation with *used to* or *didn't use to*.

Doctor: Come in, Mr Bates. Sit down. What can I do for you?

Mr Bates: I don't know doctor. I don't feel well. I _____1 feel like this.

Doctor: What's wrong?

Mr Bates: I don't know. I _____2 feel much fitter. I _____3 be able to run

for a bus and not get out of breath.

Doctor: I see.

Mr Bates: And I _____4 feel so tired. Now I feel tired all the time.

And I _____5 have this cough. Now I cough and cough and cough.

I think it's the cigarettes. Do you mind if I smoke?

Doctor: Smoke? You _____6 smoke!

Mr Bates: Yes, I did. But I didn't tell you. I _____7 smoke ten a day, but now it's about

forty a day. I worry about my health, and that makes me smoke more. Would you like a

cigarette, doctor?

Doctor: Thank you.

Mr Bates: Oh! You _____8 smoke!

Doctor: No. You're right, I didn't. I've just started!

4 The Curtiss family have moved from England to Australia. How are their lives different? Use *used to* or *didn't use to*.

England	Australia
The family lived in the city.	They live on a farm.
Emma didn't like school.	She likes her new school.
Mr Curtiss was a mechanic.	He's a farmer.
Mrs Curtiss was a typist.	She helps on the farm.
Steve Curtiss was unemployed.	He's studying at agricultural college.
They didn't have a dog.	They have three sheep dogs.
Sally, the baby, cried a lot.	She's much happier.
Emma didn't have many friends.	Now she's got lots of friends.
Mr Curtiss smoked a lot.	He doesn't smoke at all.
The weather in England wasn't good.	In Australia the weather's wonderful.
They didn't have an Australian accent.	They have strong Australian accents.
They didn't enjoy life.	They enjoy life very much.

Examples:

The family used to live in the city, but now they live on a farm.

Emma didn't use to like school, but she likes her new school.

1 _____

2 _____

3 _____

4 _____

5 _____

6 _____

7 _____

8 _____

9 _____

10 _____

5 Compare these two maps of Shillingford. What did there/didn't there use to be?

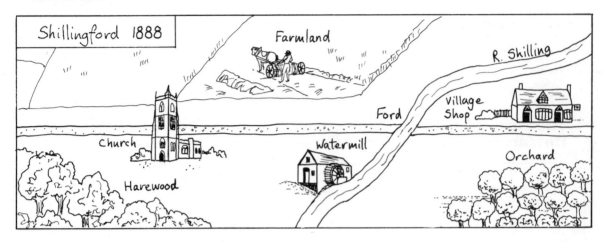

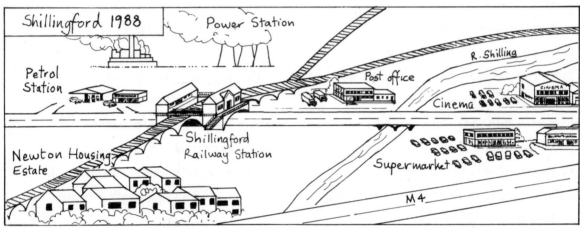

Examples:

There used to be farmland where the power station is.

There didn't use to be a power station.

1 _____

2 _____

3 _____

4 _____

5 _____

6 _____

7 _____

8 _____

9 _____

10 _____

6 What was your town like 200 years ago? What did there use to be? What didn't there use to be? Look at the box. Add two more examples. Then write sentences on the next page.

electricity	television
schools	shops
gas	supermarkets
cars	blacksmith
churches	market
cinemas	_____
horses and carts	_____
radios	

Examples:

There didn't use to be any electricity.

There used to be two schools.

1 _____
2 _____
3 _____
4 _____
5 _____
6 _____
7 _____
8 _____
9 _____
10 _____
11 _____
12 _____
13 _____
14 _____
15 _____

10

Comparison of adverbs

Comparative (regular and irregular)

fast	–	faster	early	–	earlier	well	–	better
hard	–	harder	far	–	further	badly	–	worse
high	–	higher						

	passes ball early	controls ball well	kicks ball far	jumps high	runs fast	shoots hard
Spinetti	⚽⚽	⚽⚽	⚽⚽⚽	⚽⚽	⚽	⚽
Hudson	⚽	⚽⚽⚽	⚽	⚽	⚽⚽⚽	⚽⚽⚽
Muller	⚽⚽⚽	⚽	⚽⚽	⚽⚽⚽	⚽⚽	⚽⚽

1 A Compare Spinetti with Hudson

Example:

Spinetti passes the ball earlier, kicks the ball further and jumps higher than Hudson.

Hudson controls the ball _____

_____

B Compare Spinetti with Muller

Spinetti controls the ball _____

_____

Muller passes the ball _____

_____

C Compare Hudson with Muller

Hudson controls the ball _____

_____

Muller passes the ball _____

_____

15

54

Superlative (regular and irregular)

fast – fastest	early – earliest	better – best
hard – hardest	far – furthest	worse – worse
high – highest		

2 Who do you think is 'Footballer of the Year'? Look at the table in Exercise 1. Use the superlative form of the adverb.

I think   is 'Footballer of the Year' because he _____

_____

_____

_____

_____

3 Spinetti, Hudson and Muller also have problems. Look at the table and complete.

> *Use:* **badly, worse, worst.**

	Sometimes plays badly away from home	Sometimes behaves badly on the field
Spinetti	⚽ ⚽	⚽ ⚽
Hudson	⚽	⚽ ⚽ ⚽
Muller	⚽ ⚽ ⚽	⚽

Spinetti, Hudson and Muller all play **_badly_** away from home sometimes. Spinetti plays _____1 than Hudson, and Muller plays _____2 than Spinetti. Muller certainly plays _____3 of all three away from home. Also, Hudson sometimes behaves _____4 on the field. They all behave _____5 sometimes, but Hudson behaves _____6.

Comparative *more*

Example:	carefully	– **more** carefully
	quickly	– **more** quickly
Tom works ***more carefully***	intelligently	– **more** intelligently
than Alan.	easily	– **more** easily
	deeply	– **more** deeply

	Capelli	King	Markov
Plans his moves intelligently	♟♟♟	♟	♟♟
Makes his moves quickly	♟	♟♟	♟♟♟
Thinks deeply	♟♟♟	♟♟	♟
Prepares his matches carefully	♟♟	♟♟♟	♟
Gets angry easily	♟	♟♟♟	♟♟

4 Compare the chess players. Look at the example below.

Example: Capelli

Capelli plans his moves more intelligently than King or Markov, thinks more deeply than King or Markov, and prepares his matches more carefully than Markov.

1 King

_____

_____

_____

2 Markov

_____

_____

_____

Superlative with *most*

more carefully	– (the) **most** carefully
more quickly	– (the) **most** quickly
more intelligently	– (the) **most** intelligently
more easily	– (the) **most** easily
more deeply	– (the) **most** deeply

5 Complete the conversation. Use the comparative and the superlative. Look at the table in Exercise 4.

Alan: It's an interesting world championship this year.

Sue: Yes. Three really good players: King, Markov and Capelli. I think King's the best. He prepares his matches ***more carefully*** than the others.

Alan: Yes, but he gets angry the _____1 _____2 I think Capelli will do well. Of the three, he plans his moves the _____3 _____4 and thinks _____5 _____6 _____7.

Sue: Yes, but he doesn't think very quickly. King and Markov both think _____8 _____9 than he does.

Alan: Yes, but they both get angry _____10 _____11, too.

Sue: OK, but of the three, King prepares for his matches the _____12 _____13. I think that's important.

Alan: Well, I still think Capelli's the best. He thinks the _____14 _____15, plans his moves the _____16 _____17, prepares his matches _____18 _____19 _____20 Markov and doesn't get angry easily.

Sue: Nonsense! You know nothing about chess! King is definitely the best! He . . .

6 Complete these sentences. Use the adverb in the correct comparative form + *than*

Example:

Miss Hunter understands the company (good) ***better than*** her boss.

1 Mr Johnson always arrives for work (early) _____ anyone else.

2 Karen types (careful) _____ Sally.

3 Mr Evans always leaves the office (late) _____ anyone else.

4 Miss Johnson deals with problems (efficient) _____ Mrs Harvey.

5 Miss Shaw types letters (fast) _____ before, on her new word-processor.

6 The new computer checks the files (quick) _____ we did.

7 This year's sales figures are (bad) _____ last year's.

8 The computer does everything (easy) _____ we could.

20

8

11

Possessive pronouns

my	– **mine**	our	– **ours**
your	– **yours**	your	– **yours**
his	– **his**	their	– **theirs**
her	– **hers**		

1 What are they saying? Complete with *mine, yours* etc.

Example:

Relative pronouns

Who

We use *who* when we are talking about people.

Example: He's the man **who** lives next door.

Example: Those are the girls **who** came to our party.

2 Write sentences.

Example: There's the man. He stole my bag!

> *There's the man who stole my bag!*

1 She's the woman. She phoned yesterday.

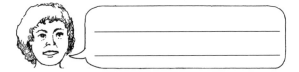

2 That's the athlete. He won the gold medal.

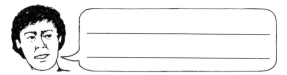

3 Where's the typist? She typed my letter.

4 That's the waiter. He served us.

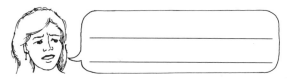

5 These are the children. They broke the window.

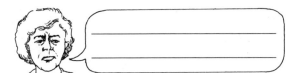

6 Where's the tourist? He lost his passport.

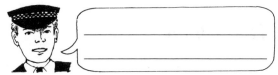

7 These are the students. They arrived today.

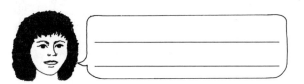

8 Are you the person? You wanted to see me.

Whose in subject and object clauses.

> There's the woman *whose* cat ran away. (Subject)
>
> That's the man *whose* dog you found. (Object)

3 Write sentences.

Examples:

She's the girl. Her brother plays for England.

She's the girl whose brother plays for England.

That's the man. I found his jacket yesterday.

That's the man whose jacket I found yesterday.

1 Those are the tourists. Their luggage arrived late.

_____

_____

2 That's the girl. I saw her photograph in the paper.

_____

_____

3 Here are the passengers. Their plane was delayed.

_____

_____

4 That's the woman. You found her passport.

_____

_____

5 That's the pop star. His record went to number one.

_____

_____

6 Those are the fishermen. Their boat sank yesterday.

_____

_____

7 Maria is the girl. Her brother is in hospital.

_____

_____

8 You're the man. I met your brother at Anna's party!

_____

_____

8

That/which

> We use *that* or *which* when we are talking about things.

4 **Tim and Pete have gone on a camping holiday, but they have a few problems! Look at the list and complete Tim's postcard. Use *that* (x3) and *which* (x2).**

LIST

1 Torch doesn't have any batteries.
2 Compass always points south.
3 Matchbox has no matches in it.
4 Boots don't fit.
5 Tin-opener works.
6 Tent doesn't let the rain in.

Dear Anna,
Camping in Wales was
not a good idea! We
have a torch that doesn't
have any batteries,

But at least we have a

Wish you were here, Tim

Anna Papadopoulou.
Metamorfoseos 62,
Kalamaria,
Thessaloniki,
Greece

We can omit *who* or *that*. Look at these sentences.

Examples: He's the teacher **I met** yesterday. (without *who*)

Where's the book **I gave** you! (without *that*)

5 Find the sentences!

Example: pen yesterday lost you here's the

Here's the pen you lost yesterday.

1 you took photographs the very good are

_____

2 the man he's saw we hotel in the

_____

3 I bought those the are chocolates?

_____

4 here's you lost the cassette

_____

5 want you Sally's see to the person

_____

6 the saw good very was doctor we

_____

7 music the disco awful at played was they the

_____

8 great we at stayed hotel the was   .

_____

6 Now write the sentences in Exercise 5 again, using *who* for people and *that* for things.

Example: ***Here's the pen that you lost yesterday.***

1 _____

2 _____

3 _____

4 _____

5 _____

6 _____

7 _____

8 _____

12

Shall/will

Affirmative

Long form		Short form	
I shall listen	we $\begin{Bmatrix} \text{shall} \\ \text{will} \end{Bmatrix}$ listen	I'll listen	we'll listen
you will listen	you will listen	you'll listen	you'll listen
he will listen	they will listen	he'll listen	they'll listen
she will listen		she'll listen	
it will listen		it'll listen	

Negative

Long form		Short form	
I shall not listen	we $\begin{Bmatrix} \text{shall not} \\ \text{will not} \end{Bmatrix}$ listen	I shan't listen	we $\begin{Bmatrix} \text{shan't} \\ \text{won't} \end{Bmatrix}$ listen
you will not listen	you will not listen	you won't listen	you won't listen
he will not listen	they will not listen	he won't listen	they won't listen
she will not listen		she won't listen	
it will not listen		it won't listen	

Predicting/promising

Example: **I'll be** in Paris on Monday.

1 **Mick Denver is trying to arrange an international pop concert for 'World Aid' on the 1st August. Who *will/won't be* there? Where *will* they be?**

> ### 1st AUGUST
>
> Ricky Clifford - OK   Girls at Work   - Athens
>
> Medusa   - New York   Rod Elton & Cliff Stewart   - OK
>
> Dry Dry Dry - OK
>
> Princess   - Rome   Sara and the Royals   - Paris
>
> Nanarama   - OK   Charlie and the Wailers   - OK
>
> Red Red Red - Moscow

Examples: **Ricky Clifford will be there.**

         Medusa won't be there. She'll be in New York.

1 _____

2 _____

3 _____

4 _____

5 _____

6 _____

7 _____

8 _____

Questions		Short answers
Shall I listen?	Shall we listen?	Yes, he will.
Will you listen?	Will you listen?	No, they won't.
Will he/she/it listen?	Will they listen?	

2 Look back at the list in Exercise 1. Write sentences.

Examples:

A: *Will Ricky Clifford be there?*

B: *Yes, he will.*

A: *Will Medusa be there?*

B: *No, she won't. She won't be there.*

1 A: _____

  B: _____

2 A: _____

  B: _____

3 A: _____

  B: _____

4 A: _____

  B: _____

5 A: _____

  B: _____

6 A: _____

  B: _____

7 A: _____

  B: _____

8 A: _____

  B: _____

3 Professor Hartford is giving a television interview about the space ship *Explorer 10*. Complete with *will* or *won't*.

Interviewer: Professor Hartford. *Explorer 10* leaves tomorrow for Pluto. When **will** it land?

How long _____ **1** the journey take?

Hartford: It _____ **2** take two years to get to Pluto.

Interviewer: And what do you expect to find when you get there? _____ **3** there be life on Pluto?

Hartford: We can't be sure. There _____ **4** be any *human* life, but there may be other forms.

We _____ **5** know until we get there.

Interviewer: And the four astronauts, what _____ **6** they do during the two-year trip?

Professor: Well, we hope they _____ **7** be too bored. They _____ **8** have to check their instruments and keep physically and mentally fit. We hope they _____ **9** still like each other after two years!

Interviewer: Thank you very much, Professor Hartford. We _____ **10** talk to you again in two years' time. Good luck to *Explorer 10*!

Present continuous (future meaning) —————

Arrangements

4 The Sanchez family are going on holiday to England next week. What are their arrangements? Complete Maria's letter to her friends in Cambridge. Use the present continuous.

Calle de la Rosa, 26
Salamanca,
30ᵗʰ September.

Dear Sally and Tom,

I hope you and the family are well. We're looking forward very much to our visit to England. We (leave) **'re leaving** Madrid at ten o'clock on Monday and (arrive) _____¹ at Heathrow at twelve o'clock. We (stay) _____² at the Royal Hotel in Victoria. Do you know it? Some friends told us it was good, but not very expensive.

We (plan) _____³ to visit lots of interesting places in London. On Tuesday we (go) _____⁴ to Windsor Castle and on Wednesday we (visit) _____⁵ the Tower of London. We also wanted to see a musical, so we've booked to see 'Cats'. On Thursday we (go) _____⁶ by train to Oxford to visit the colleges. I know you and Tom studied at Cambridge, so we hope to visit Cambridge University on Friday. We (arrive) _____⁷ at about nine p.m.

Thank you again for offering us a bed on Friday evening. We (fly) _____⁸ back to Madrid on Saturday 6ᵗʰ, so it's just for one night.

See you soon,
Love from us all.

65

5 Look at Doctor Hamilton's notes and complete the conversation.

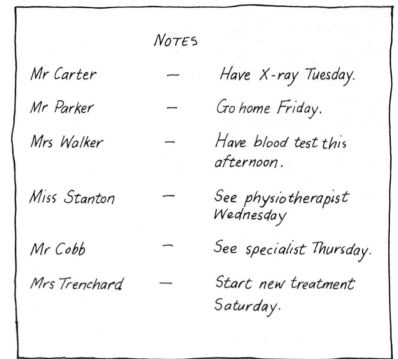

NOTES

Mr Carter	—	Have X-ray Tuesday.
Mr Parker	—	Go home Friday.
Mrs Walker	—	Have blood test this afternoon.
Miss Stanton	—	See physiotherapist Wednesday
Mr Cobb	—	See specialist Thursday.
Mrs Trenchard	—	Start new treatment Saturday.

Example: So, Mr Carter/have his X-ray Monday.

Dr. Trent: ***So, Mr Carter's having his X-ray on Monday.***

Dr. Hamilton: ***No, he isn't. That's Tuesday. He isn't having his X-ray until Tuesday.***

1 Mr Parker/go home on Wednesday.

Dr. Trent: _____

Dr. Hamilton: _____

2 Mrs Walker/have her blood test this morning.

Dr. Trent: _____

Dr. Hamilton: _____

3 Miss Stanton/see the physiotherapist on Monday.

Dr. Trent: _____

Dr. Hamilton: _____

4 Mr. Cobb/see a specialist on Tuesday.

Dr. Trent: _____

Dr. Hamilton: _____

5 Mrs. Trenchard/start new treatment on Thursday.

Dr. Trent: _____

10

Dr. Hamilton: _____

6 Now complete this conversation between Dr. Hamilton and his patients. Look at the notes in Exercise 5.

Example: Mr. Carter/X-ray Monday.

Mr Carter: ***Am I having my X-ray on Monday?***

Dr. Hamilton: ***No.***

Mr Carter: ***When am I having it then?***

Dr. Hamilton: ***On Tuesday.***

1 Mr Parker/go home Wednesday.

Mr Parker: _____

Dr. Hamilton: _____

Mr Parker: _____

Dr. Hamilton: _____

2 Mrs Walker/blood test this morning.

Mrs Walker: _____

Dr. Hamilton: _____

Mrs Walker: _____

Dr. Hamilton: _____

3 Miss Stanton/see physiotherapist Monday.

Miss Stanton: _____

Dr. Hamilton: _____

Miss Stanton: _____

Dr. Hamilton: _____

4 Mr Cobb/see specialist Tuesday.

Mr Cobb: _____

Dr. Hamilton: _____

Mr Cobb: _____

Dr. Hamilton: _____

5 Mrs Trenchard/start new treatment Thursday.

Mrs Trenchard: _____

Dr. Hamilton: _____

Mrs Trenchard: _____

Dr. Hamilton: _____

13

Present simple (future meaning)

When, until, as soon as, before

> *Examples:*
>
> I'll **send** you a postcard │ when │ I **arrive** in New York.
>
> │ When │ I **arrive** in New York, I'**ll send** you a postcard.

1 Look at the example and complete the sentences.

Example:

I (phone) *'ll phone* them when I (get) *get* to Paris.

1 We (wait) _____ here until the rain (stop) _____.

2 As soon as the match (end) _____ we (complain) _____ to the referee.

3 I (stay) _____ with you until your train (leave) _____.

4 She (worry) _____ about her exam until she (get) _____ the results.

5 As soon as Dad (get) _____ in tonight he (want) _____ his dinner.

6 We (not start) _____ lunch until you (get) _____ back.

7 When Peter (arrive) _____ we (give) _____ him his presents.

8 When the exam (be) _____ over we (have) _____ a party.

9 I (have) _____ an ice-cream before the film (start) _____.

10 I finish _____ this book before I (go) _____ to bed.

2 Mrs Fullbright is having the last driving lesson before her test. What does she say she will do on the day of the test?

Example: a) get   b) will get

I'll put on my glasses before I ***get*** in the car.

1 a) put   b) 'll put

As soon as I get in the car I _____ on my seat belt.

2 a) start   b) will start

I'll check the driving mirror before I _____ .

3 a) don't leave   b) won't leave

When I drive off I _____ the handbrake on.

4 a) tells   b) will tell

I won't look at the examiner when he _____ me to turn right or left.

5 a) put on   b) will put on

When I stop at traffic lights I _____ the handbrake.

6 a) reverse   b) will reverse

I'll go slowly when I _____.

7 a) asks   b) will ask

I won't turn left or right unless the examiner _____ me to.

8 a) signal   b) 'll signal

Before I turn left or right I _____.

9 a) says   b) will say

I'll stop as soon as the instructor _____ 'Stop'.

10 a) come   b) will come

I'll slow down when I _____ to a roundabout.

---

3 Look at the verbs in the box and complete these sentences. Look at the example below.

open   break down   stay   be   leave   send
(wait)   go   cook
get   sell   see   come
arrive   land   (stop)   phone   type

Example: We*'ll wait* until the rain *stops*.

1 They _____ us when they _____ at Heathrow.

2 They _____ us a note before they _____ for Paris.

3 I (not) _____ my presents until everyone _____ here.

4 As soon as we _____ home I _____ the dinner.

5 We _____ the car before it _____.

6 We _____ Madonna when she _____ to London.

7 We _____ here until the police _____.

8 I _____ one more letter before I _____ home.

First conditional

If you *give* me your address, I'*ll write* to you.
If you *don't leave* now, you'*ll miss* your train.
OR
I'*ll write* to you if you *give* me your address.
You'*ll miss* your train if you *don't leave* now.

4 Make sentences. Look at the example below.

If Jenny gets a new job.	she'll buy a new one.
If Nick buys a car	he won't be here for my birthday.
It it rains	he'll be near the station.
If John gets up at eight o'clock	I'll lose weight.
If they don't work hard.	he won't have enough money to go on holiday.
If she loses her umbrella	we'll drive to the party.
If I don't eat biscuits	he'll be late for work.
If Jim moves house	she'll meet interesting people.
If my brother goes to France this summer	they won't pass their exams.

Example:

If Nick buys a car he won't have enough money to go on holiday.

1 _____
2 _____
3 _____
4 _____
5 _____
6 _____
7 _____
8 _____

5 Complete the sentences.

Example:

If we (go) **go** to the cinema, we (miss) **'ll miss** the football match on television.

1 If Italy (score) _____ again, they (win) _____ 3:0.

2 Manuella (come) _____ to your party, if you (ask) _____ her.

3 You (play) _____ better, if you (practise) _____ more.

4 If I (lend) _____ you my bike, you (fall) _____ off it.

5 If they (not come) _____ soon, the party (be) _____ over.

8

6 He (not get) _____ a good job, if he (not pass) _____ his exams.

7 If the train (be) _____ late, we (not catch) _____ our plane.

8 We (have) _____ a great time, if we (go) _____ to Acapulco!

6 Carol is riding a bicycle for the first time. What are her problems?

Example: try to stop/fall off

If she tries to stop, she'll fall off.

1 jump off/hurt herself.

_____

_____

2 ring the bell/no one hear her.

_____

_____

3 turn left/run over the children.

_____

_____

4 turn right/crash into the lorry.

_____

_____

5 not do anything/go into the pond.

_____

_____

6 go into pond/get very wet.

_____

_____

7 not do something soon/be too late.

_____

_____

8 stop in time/be a miracle!

_____

_____

14

Must/have to (have got to)

MUST: I **must** write to Andreas.	HAVE TO: We **have to** ⎫ take an exam
(*You* decide.)	we**'ve got to** ⎭
	(*Somebody else* decides.)

1 Write sentences. Look at the examples.

Example:

I **must** clean the car.

Example:

I**'ve got to** clean the car.

1

We _____ work late this evening.

2

I _____ mend this hosepipe.

3

We _____ cut the grass.

4

I _____ tidy my room.

5 We _____ do something about that noise.

6 The doctor says I _____ go into hospital tomorrow.

7 I _____ get some food before the shops close.

8 I _____ do the washing up.

Questions

Do I/you have to . . .?	When do I have to . . .?
Have I/you got to . . .?	Where have I got to . . .?

2 Write the other form.

Examples: Do we have to hand in our passports at the hotel?

Have we got to hand in our passports at the hotel?

Why have we got to be there so early?

Why do we have to be there so early?

1 Why have I got to be home by ten o'clock?

_____

2 Do we have to tell Sue?

_____

3 Does he have to walk to work?

_____

4 When have we got to leave?

_____

5 Do you have to work at weekends?

_____

6 Who has she got to ask, then?

_____

7 When have they got to book their tickets?

_____

8 Where do I have to wait?

_____

Should/ought to ══════════════════════════

He	should	work harder.
	ought to	

3 Match the sentences. Choose one sentence from the 'situation' box and one from the 'advice' box. Use *should* (x5) and *ought to* (x5)

Situation	Advice
Tom's ill.	buy a new one
Emma is worried about her exams.	phone the bank
1 Paula's got toothache.	wait until his birthday
2 Tessa and Carol are late for work.	see a doctor
3 Mrs Roberts can see a man climbing in through her neighbour's window.	have an eye-test
4 Amanda has lost her cheque book.	go to bed earlier
5 Alan wakes up tired every morning.	go to the dentist
6 Mrs Adams can't see very well.	take more exercise
7 Tom's car breaks down at least once a week.	work harder
8 Mr Barclay is getting too fat.	phone the police
9 Mario wants to open his present now.	drive more carefully
10 Mr Williams had an accident in his car yesterday. He was going too fast.	leave immediately

Examples:

Tom's ill.

Emma is worried about her exams.

He ought to see a doctor.

She should work harder.

1 _____

2 _____

74

3 _____

4 _____

5 _____

6 _____

7 _____

8 _____

9 _____

10 _____

Shouldn't/oughtn't to

4 Helena is taking some important exams tomorrow. What *should* or *shouldn't* she do?

Example: panic

She shouldn't panic.

1 read the questions carefully

_____

2 write too much

_____

3 answer all the questions

_____

4 write clearly

_____

5 cheat

_____

5 Pete has an interview for a job tomorrow. What *ought* or *oughtn't* he to do?

Example: think about the job before the interview.

He ought to think about the job before the interview.

1 prepare some questions to ask

_____

2 put on a smart suit

_____

3 worry too much

_____

4 have a haircut

_____

5 be late

_____

6 Daniella and Graziella are going to England for two months to learn English. It's November. What *should* they do or *oughtn't* they to do?

Example: pack plenty of warm clothes.

They should pack plenty of warm clothes.

1 choose a good language school.

_____

2 speak Italian when they get to England.

_____

3 spend too much money in the first month.

_____

4 write to or phone their families every week.

_____

5 take their umbrellas!

_____

15

Reflexive verbs

I hurt **myself**	we hurt **ourselves**
you hurt **yourself**	you hurt **yourselves**
he hurts **himself**	they hurt **themselves**
she hurts **herself**	
it hurts **itself**	

It's OK, I haven't hurt myself.

1 Complete these sentences.

Example: We've hurt **_ourselves_**.

1 I hurt _____ playing football yesterday.

2 Don't cut _____ ,Tom.

3 It's OK. Bill and Roger haven't hurt _____ .

4 Our cat fell fifty feet out of a tree, but it didn't hurt _____ .

5 Careful! We mustn't burn _____ .

6 Paula! Chris! Be careful! You'll hurt _____ .

7 Ella eats and eats. She can't stop _____ .

8 Mr Edwards fell down three times last week, but he didn't even bruise _____ .

2 Match the sentences with the pictures.

Example:

She's burnt herself on the iron.

Paul's cut himself shaving.

Andreas is teaching himself English.

Don't hurt yourselves on those new skateboards.

Colin's cut himself on the glass.

She's burnt herself on the iron.

You've bruised yourself badly.

The climber couldn't stop himself.

1

_____

_____

2

_____

_____

3

_____

_____

4

_____

5

_____

6

_____

3 Complete the newspaper headlines.

Use:
**teach,
burn,
stop,
enjoy,
throw**
+ a reflexive
pronoun

Man *throws himself* off skyscraper

Fire eater _____ !
"I couldn't _____ "
says murderer

Fourteen-year-old boy _____ Chinese in 3 months!

" _____ while you're young," says Cecil Grant — 100 years old today!

Phrasal verbs

Examples: He **is putting** his coat **on**.

They **are plugging** the television **in**.

She is **picking** it **up**.

4 Look at the phrasal verbs in the box and match them with the pictures. Use the present continuous.

Example:

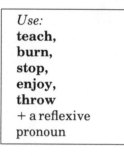

put	away	plug	off
light	television	iron	on
pullover	coat	in	records
up	take	switch	
pick	letters		

He's taking his pullover off.

1

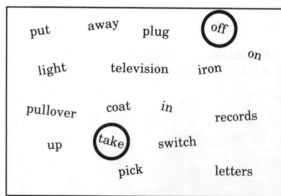

_____

2

_____

_____

_____

_____

_____

_____

_____

_____

_____

5 Now make six conversations like these. Use your answers to numbers 1–6 in Exercise 4 to help you.

Example:

Mrs Edwards: **_Take your pullover off!_**

Richard: **_I've taken it off._**

1 Mrs Bates: _____

   Mr Bates: _____

2 Mr Grant: _____

   Mrs Grant: _____

3 Bill: _____

   Kate: _____

4 Mrs Clark: _____

   Mr Clark: _____

5 Mrs Stanton: _____

   Mr Stanton: _____

6 Mrs Edwards: _____

   Peter and Sara: _____

6 What did Mrs Evans do when she heard the burglar downstairs?

> *Use:* **come in, drive away, fall down, get up, go away, jump out, run away, sit down, wake up** and the past simple

Mrs Evans **woke up** at three o'clock in the morning. There was a man downstairs.

She _____ 1, got dressed and phoned the police. Then she hid behind the door and waited.

Slowly the door opened. Suddenly Mrs Evans _____ 2 and shouted: "_____ 3!

I've phoned the police!" She pushed the burglar out of the room and he _____ 4 the stairs.

Then the police _____ 5 and caught the man before he could _____ 6.

They then _____ 7 with the burglar in their car to the police station, and Mrs Evans

_____ 8 and made herself a nice cup of tea!

8

7 The Taylor family are moving house. Complete the conversation with: *off, away, down, in, up, on.*

Mr Taylor: Be careful with that chair, Sally. Don't bring it **in** yet. And don't try to pick that

table _____ 1. It's too heavy.

Nick: Can I turn the television _____ 2, Dad? Italy are playing Spain.

Dad: No . . . and don't sit _____ 3 the fridge. You'll fall _____ 4.

Mrs Taylor: Where are the car keys? Has anyone picked them _____ 5?

Sally: Oh, look! I've found my records!

Mr Taylor: Not now, Sally. Put them _____ 6 . . . And get _____ 7 the sofa.

Nick: Oh, no. It's started to rain.

Mrs Taylor: It's OK. We've finished. Everything's inside. Let's sit _____ 8 and have a
cup of coffee!

8